T0195002

INVEST in CANCER STOCKS

MAKE MONEY AND MAKE A DIFFERENCE

Eric Shea Broadus

WESTBOW
PRESS®
A DIVISION OF THOMAS NELSON
& ZONDERVAN

WestBow Press books may be ordered through booksellers or by contacting:

WestBow Press
A Division of Thomas Nelson & Zondervan
1663 Liberty Drive
Bloomington, IN 47403
www.westbowpress.com
844-714-3454

Scripture quotations marked NIV are taken from The Holy Bible, New International Version®, NIV® Copyright © 1973, 1978, 1984, 2011 by Biblica, Inc.® Used by permission. All rights reserved worldwide.

ISBN: 978-1-6642-8790-7 (sc)
ISBN: 978-1-6642-8791-4 (hc)
ISBN: 978-1-6642-8789-1 (e)

Library of Congress Control Number: 2022923806

Print information available on the last page.

WestBow Press rev. date: 01/18/2023

CONTENTS

ACKNOWLEDGMENTS

This book is a seed that is finally ready to be planted. As I do so, I have so many to thank for this opportunity.

First and foremost, I dedicate this book to my Lord and Savior, Jesus Christ. I am who I am, or ever will become, because of the Great I AM.

Next, I want to thank my dear wife, Liliana (I call her Carolina), for her steadfast love for me. She added enormous creativity and thoughtfulness in helping me finish this book. It is beyond words how much I love and appreciate her. I love you, Amor.

I want to thank my parents, Eric Norris Broadus and Olivia Denise Stowers, and my parents-in-law, Hector and Ilse Perez, for their love and support. Also, I would like to express my most heartfelt appreciation to my aunt Lillian Charleston and my uncle William Henry Broadus for their many words of encouragement over the years.

I am also grateful to David Williams, my former boss at a company I worked for in Duluth, Georgia and Ron Cox, a Christian men's fellowship leader at Gwinnet Church in Sugar Hill, Georgia. They took time out of their busy days to read drafts of the manuscript. I appreciate knowing these great men of faith.

Finally, I extend "love you and respect you" sentiments to all cancer patients, cancer survivors, and those deceased because of cancer, including many in my family, my wife's family, and friends. They have touched my life and have inspired me to write this book.

INTRODUCTION

From Heartbreak to a Great Discovery

There is never a shortage of soul-inspiring stories that can ignite the flames within—stories that arouse a person's keen impulses and curiosities to strive for higher heights despite experiencing on occasion the most unfair of circumstances. What I am about to share with you is surely no different. It is about an extremely ambitious young man who grew up in his hometown of Indianapolis, Indiana. He was a good student whose high school grades and extracurricular activities (including being student-body president his senior year) were good enough for him to earn admission and a scholarship as a biology/premed major to a highly reputable, private, in-state institution of higher learning, Butler University. The future looked bright for him as he set out to fulfill his childhood dream of one day becoming a medical doctor.

About four weeks into his first semester, he began to experience moments of intense fatigue compounded by a series of back-to-back colds and flu-like illnesses that materialized in similar fashion to a perfect array of vertical dominos lined up on a table and subsequently falling over one another within a brief period. By early October of that semester, this young man was missing all classes, staying home to recover. He knew something was not right, but—as many bright-eyed yet immature eighteen-year-olds would do—brushed it off as a common, insignificant setback. *No big deal,* he thought. Ignoring those warning signs would cost him dearly a few weeks later—with unimaginable downstream consequences that would span multiple years. Still battling annoying flu-like symptoms, and on occasion noticing trickles of blood appearing from blowing his nose after a sneeze, he made the determination to return to his classes on campus.

On one of those unremarkable routine days, he was sitting uncomfortably in biology class, struggling to listen to the professor's lecture, when he suddenly began to feel the most powerful, violent sensations of nausea and stomach cramps that he had ever felt in his life. There is simply no other way to describe it than this: he felt like he needed to vomit and defecate at the same time. In that unexpected instance of experiencing those sharp pains, he jumped up from his classroom seat and, startling his classmates a bit, ran as fast as he could toward the exit to reach the men's restroom a few feet away before the biological inevitable was to occur.

He never made it to the men's restroom.

When he opened his eyes, the young college student had a panoramic view of the hallway ceiling and images of strange men in blurry, bizarre-looking uniforms peering down at him uttering undiscernible, muffled words that sounded like the inconspicuous elementary school teacher from the classic cartoon, Charlie Brown. As he gained consciousness (for he had crashed the back of his head into the university main building hallway floor and passed out), he recognized that those strange men were paramedics who had been called to assist. After a few minutes of posing questions as he remained on the floor, they were eventually able to get the young man (now somewhat embarrassed) onto a stretcher and transport him to Methodist Hospital (as was the name back then)—the largest hospital near downtown Indianapolis—where the emergency room unit team ran a gamut of tests to determine what could be the issue.

During this time, the hospital notified his parents of the tragic occurrence, and they joined their son at the hospital later that day. After completing a series of blood tests, the doctors discovered that his white blood cell count level (i.e., leukocytes that fight infections) was astronomically high, well above normal levels. In tandem, his red blood cell count (which carries hemoglobin that transports oxygen in the blood) and platelets cell count (which prevents internal and external bleeding) were significantly below normal levels. The rapid, irregular production of unhealthy white blood cells were crowding out the typically normal production of red blood cells and platelets—thus the reason for the nosebleeds when sneezing and eventually collapsing to the university hallway floor due to lack of adequate oxygen to the brain.

After completing a series of additional medical exams, the results were conclusive to the doctors. The doctors diagnosed the young college student with a fully advanced stage of acute myeloid leukemia (AML), the deadliest form of leukemia known to humans at that time, and surprisingly common in children up to eighteen years old. Given the severity of his current condition, the doctors were doubtful that he would survive more than a few days and subtly informed his parents that they should consider making those awful, dreaded preparations that no parent is ever ready to make. Beyond the obvious health concerns, the heartbreak of the young man having to leave school, while his friends moved on with their lives, was devastating.

Truly fortunate for him, that was not the end of the story. God had other plans.

After a series of extremely aggressive chemotherapy and radiation treatments, and some other severely trying, near-death episodes that occurred over several months, he eventually became a prime candidate to receive a bone marrow transplant from one of his two younger sisters and spent the next three years in recovery in and out of outpatient care. That young man went on to graduate from great universities (Indiana University-Purdue University Indianapolis (IUPUI) and Johns Hopkins University), travel around the globe, and work for world-renowned organizations in the various areas of international finance, healthcare finance, and foreign currency risk management. He is married to a wonderful, sweet lady originally born in Colombia, South America, who became a US citizen many years ago. That young man after thirty years now has speckles of gray in his hair.

As you have probably figured out by now, that young man in the story is me, the author of this book.

After finalizing my treatment and completing my formal education, I spent several valuable years in the corporate world working in various finance jobs related to global cash management, international treasury, and healthcare finance that included a stint as finance manager at the Johns Hopkins Department of Pediatric Oncology. As a sort of a hobby, I became increasingly interested in researching and investing in companies that play a significant role in fighting cancer. I turned my hobby (a quite successful one) into a true passion and obtained my professional investment advisor license. I developed a deep passion for investing in stocks and possessed an unapologetic desire to reap the financial rewards for doing so.

A lingering, unquenchable question frequently came to my mind as I experienced the joys embedded within my hobby. *How many people who hate cancer as much as (or even more than) I do would love to receive professional guidance and advice on how to invest in companies fighting cancer?* That question remained vibrant and is as relevant to me today as it was many years ago. I concluded that it was time to do more than just pose the question. It was time to find some solutions.

I want to inspire, educate, and steer individual investors toward the most profitable investment opportunities related to preventing, diagnosing, and fighting the most prolific forms of cancer. I decided to form a company called Can Serve Free LLC as a unique, highly specialized investment advisory firm. The business name sounds unmistakably like *cancer free*, yes? That was no coincidence. I'll discuss more about the services of Can Serve Free LLC near the end of the book.

I intentionally limited the focus and scope of this book. It is not an all-encompassing book on cancer from a clinical or academic perspective. Medical science researchers would always do a better job than me in describing the biological constructs and impacts of cancer. This book does not cover in detail the fabulous work of specific hospitals or other not-for-profit organizations dedicated to the global fight against cancer. Many writers have done an exceptional job covering the valiant efforts of organizations such as St. Jude, the American Cancer Society, the Leukemia-Lymphoma Society, CancerCare, the World Cancer Research Fund International, and others. I have the deepest respect and admiration for such organizations and would encourage everyone to consider giving or increasing their charitable donations to them.

I penned this book with you, the profit-seeking investor, squarely in mind. You are ambitious and remarkably busy, yet thoughtful and conscientious, and want to leave behind a legacy for others to follow. You love making money without apology and the freedom it provides, and you equally hate cancer in all its diabolical forms and effects. This book was written for you, an investor who has a spectrum of experiences. Perhaps you are a new or experienced investor with a general aversion to the perils of cancer who knows a few people directly affected. Or perhaps you are an investor who has a personal disdain for a particular type of cancer from either direct experience or having a friend or loved one who has or had that type of cancer. The common bond for all readers that I am seeking to reach is your desire to build profitable investment portfolios that add new streams of wealth and financial success. Many of you would love to learn how to invest in cancer stocks, identify the best investment opportunities, and pass on your purchased assets (while alive or after passing away) to loved ones. If any of the above details describe you, then this book is for you.

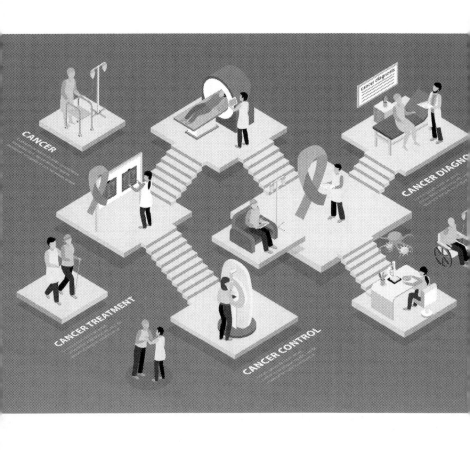

CANCER

CANCER DIAGNO

CANCER TREATMENT

CANCER CONTROL

CHAPTER ONE

Screening and Prevention Made the Difference

Prevention is better than cure.
—**Desiderius Erasmus, sixteenth-century Dutch philosopher**

The battle against cancer is lifelong. A few decades after my first encounter with cancer, I noticed from time to time some blood in the toilet after using the bathroom. I did not pay much attention because I knew that I had some hemorrhoids in a not-so-strategic place that also bled on occasion when I was a tad too aggressive with the toilet paper. Enough said. My wife would occasionally notice some blood on the toilet and told me in a not-so-subtle posture and tone that I needed to see a doctor.

"Ho hum. It's time for my annual physical," I said to myself. "I hate going to those things … total waste of time and money. Just giving my doctor more money for him to use to put another addition onto his huge house [which I had never seen before, of course] or a few more dollars for him to go play golf [complete bias on my part assuming all doctors play golf]." It is obvious that I did not have the best attitude about going to such an appointment. Ignorance and arrogance can often lead to perilous consequences if one is not careful. Proverbs 16:18 (NIV version) from the Holy

Bible says, "Pride goes before destruction, a haughty spirit before a fall."

This annual physical exam would prove to be quite different from all other annual exams I have had over the multiple decades of my life. My doctor came into the room without even saying hello to me and simply blurted out, "Eric, you're getting up in age now. How do you want to get your colon examined?"

I said, "What?"

He said, "Yep, it's time for a thorough review of your insides! Do you want it done the invasive way or the noninvasive way?"

Not in a million years would I have *ever* said to him, "Yeah, Doc, let's go the invasive route." I said as politely as I could, without giving him a direct scowl, "Sure, let's go the noninvasive route."

From my directive, he ordered a colon cancer screening package called Cologuard (produced by Exact Sciences Corporation) that was subsequently mailed to my house. Upon receiving the package and reading the instructions a few days later, I proceeded to do the "number two" into a container placed over the toilet seat, poured a clear liquid chemical into the container with the waste, sealed the opening containing the feces and liquid, placed labels with my name on the container, put the container in a large plastic bag, dropped the plastic bag into a prepared box, taped the box shut, applied mailing address labels on the box, and drove to a nearby UPS Store for same-day shipping. The results would be available within one week.

No problem.

Or so I thought.

Did I mention that pride comes before destruction?

One week later, a nurse from my doctor's office called and told me the results of the Cologuard test: *positive*. "Positive?" I responded to the nurse with vernacular slang like Arnold from the old 1980s TV sitcom show *Diff'rent Strokes*. "What you talkin' about? What does that mean? I feel perfectly healthy!" My doctor sent a referral to a gastroenterologist to complete a colonoscopy a few weeks later.

It turned out that I had to have that invasive colonoscopy after all. Hindsight is truly twenty/twenty.

Anyone who has ever had a colonoscopy understands what I am about to say. It is truly a horrible experience, and I say that euphemistically. The night before the procedure, one is instructed to chug down what seems like gallons of stool softeners and antibiotics to clean out the intestines. You spend the night jumping in and out of bed—compliments of those stool softeners and antibiotics. You get the point. The day of the actual colonoscopy is straightforward. They apply anesthesia via an IV, and the doctor proceeds to review your colon to detect for polyps (small tumors) that require removal same day. Easy-peasy.

However, in my case, that was not what happened. There was a problem. No, correction. There was a *huge* problem.

When I woke up from my procedure, my wife was staring at me with a serious look on her face. The seven (yes, seven) polyps that the doctor was able to remove were noncancerous. Thank God. However, he told my wife that there was an exceptionally large tumor sitting in my colon that he could not remove. It had to be surgically extracted along with the surrounding tissues (including my appendix) so that biopsies could be completed to detect for the possibility of cancer.

A few weeks later, I had the major surgery called a robotic-assisted partial colectomy that removed the tumor, a portion of my colon, the surrounding tissue, and my appendix. I had to take off a month from work to recover. The surgery was a success, and it turned out that the large tumor and surrounding tissues were also noncancerous. Praise God.

However, I received news that was slightly chilling. The doctor told me that had I not had this procedure to remove the large tumor when I did, it would have most likely led to a different story the following year. In this case, I was extremely fortunate that my primary care physician was very direct with me and told me to get my colon examined. In a real sense—despite the extremely uncomfortable experiences that occurred over those months—I thank God for using my primary care physician and other doctors. Catching these tumors early saved my life. As the commercials on TV say, if you're forty-five or older, get your colon screened for cancer. It could save your life.

That was my experience as a patient. Putting on my investment advisor's hat, I am intrigued by the opportunities people have to invest in companies that develop tools and devices designed to screen for and hopefully prevent cancer. Multicancer early detection (MCED) tools are tests that measure biological signals in body fluids that cancer cells shed. These signals are also known as biomarkers or tumor markers. Recent next-generation sequencing and machine learning advances have enabled the development of multicancer early detection tests. These are single tests that can identify a signal for many cancers from a single blood draw. They look for circulating tumor cells, tumor DNA, and other substances that might be present in several distinct types of cancer. MCED tests screen for cancers from more than one organ site at the same time and analyze DNA that has been shed by all cells, including cancer cells, into the bloodstream. Such tests look for abnormal patterns on those DNA fragments that indicate the presence of cancer and can accurately predict the part of the body from which that cancer originated. Clearly this is a very lucrative field of oncological science that investors should strongly consider when looking to build their investment portfolios. Preventative care is big business. We will return to this topic a little later in the book.

CHAPTER TWO

It's Personal, and It's Business

If we buy the business as a business and not as a stock speculation, then it becomes personal. I want it to be personal.
—Philip Bradley Town, contemporary American investor, motivational speaker, and author

Most people know someone who has had cancer, has cancer, or has unfortunately lost the earthly battle against the dreaded disease. If you were to close your eyes for thirty seconds, I am sure you could put together a list of celebrities who have passed away over the years from one of its various forms. Below is a list of famous people who quickly come to my mind.

- ➤ Beau Biden, son of President Joe Biden, died of brain cancer.
- ➤ Chadwick Boseman, whose leading roles in *Black Panther* and *42* (the story of Jackie Robinson) transcended both culture and race, died of colon cancer.
- ➤ Celia Cruz (La Guarachera de Cuba), world-famous Cuban singer, died of brain cancer.
- ➤ Lois Evans, the wife of megachurch pastor and prolific author Dr. Tony Evans, died of bile duct cancer.

- Aretha Franklin, legendary soul and gospel music singer and actor, died of pancreatic cancer.
- Joe Frazier (a.k.a. "Smokin' Joe"), former boxing heavyweight champion of the world, died of liver cancer.
- Leila Janah, up-and-coming global social entrepreneur and author who founded Sama (formerly Samasource) and LXMI, died of epithelioid sarcoma.
- Peter Jennings, former ABC World News anchor, died of lung cancer.
- Steve Jobs, cultural business icon, founder, and visionary of Apple Computer, died of pancreatic cancer.
- Ted Kennedy, former senator from the state of Massachusetts and brother of the late President John F. Kennedy, died of brain cancer.
- Coretta Scott King, beloved wife of civil rights leader/preacher Dr. Martin Luther King Jr., died of ovarian cancer.
- John Lewis, world-renowned civil rights leader and congressman for the state of Georgia, died of pancreatic cancer.
- Rush Limbaugh, nationally syndicated conservative radio talk-show host and prolific bestselling author, died of lung cancer.
- John McCain, former Arizona senator and US presidential candidate, died of brain cancer.
- Gordon S. Murray, former investment banker at Goldman Sachs, Credit Suisse First Boston, and Lehman Brothers and co-author of the New York Times bestselling book *The Investment Answer, Learn to Manage Your Money & Protect Your Financial Future*, died from glioblastoma, a type of brain cancer.
- Olivia Newton-John, a beloved actor/singer who touched the world with her performance in the theatric/TV musical *Grease*, died of breast cancer.
- Jacqueline Kennedy Onassis, former first lady and wife of President John F. Kennedy, and later married to Greek billionaire Aristotle Onassis, died of non-Hodgkin lymphoma.

> ➤ Dr. MaLinda Sapp, professor, wife, and business manager of world-renowned gospel music recording artist Marvin Sapp, died of colon cancer.
> ➤ Vidal Sassoon, British American hairstylist/entrepreneur who created and marketed women's hair products around the world, died of leukemia.
> ➤ Stuart Scott, famous ESPN sportscaster, died of appendix cancer.
> ➤ Alex Trebek, former host of the popular TV game show *Jeopardy*, died of pancreatic cancer.
> ➤ Jim Valvano ("Jimmy V"), famous basketball coach and broadcaster, who inspired millions in the fight against cancer, died of adenocarcinoma, a type of glandular cancer.

The list goes on and on and will unfortunately grow longer with each passing year. What we hope is that the cancer mortality rate will continue to decline over time.

But with all due respect to those great celebrities and leaders I mentioned above—or in deference to any other luminary for that matter—nothing comes close to the trauma we experience when it is you, your family member, or your friend who is battling cancer. It's personal. It hurts. That feeling of initial helplessness is frustrating. I've been there. You've been there. You feel it deeply and want to do something about it.

I really, *really* hate cancer. How about you?

The types of cancer prevalent today are as vast as the integral parts that make up the human body. However, there are certain cancers that should garner our attention as investors, most notably

> ➤ bladder cancer (blue, yellow, or purple ribbon)
> ➤ bone cancer (yellow ribbon)
> ➤ brain cancer (gray ribbon)
> ➤ breast cancer (pink ribbon)
> ➤ carcinoma (zebra print ribbon)

- cervical cancer (white and teal ribbon)
- colorectal cancer (dark-blue ribbon)
- head and neck cancers (white and burgundy ribbon)
- Hodgkin lymphoma (violet ribbon)
- kidney (renal) cancer (orange ribbon)
- leukemia (orange ribbon)
- liver cancer (emerald-green ribbon)
- lung cancer (white or pearl ribbon)
- multiple myeloma (burgundy ribbon)
- non-Hodgkin lymphoma (lime-green ribbon)
- oral cavity and oropharyngeal cancer (blue enamel ribbon)
- ovarian cancer (teal ribbon)
- pancreatic cancer (purple ribbon)
- prostate cancer (light-blue ribbon)
- sarcoma (yellow ribbon)
- skin cancer (black ribbon)
- stomach (gastric) cancer (periwinkle ribbon)
- thyroid cancer (blue, pink, or teal ribbon)
- testicular cancer (light-purple ribbon)
- uterine cancer (peach ribbon)

Beyond the nostalgia and emotional determination to end cancer, it is wise to face the reality of what currently confronts us. Cancer impacts the entire world, and it hits the developed world particularly hard. Countries often celebrated for their vast economic prowess and productivity achievements also share some of the highest rates of cancer worldwide, most notably Australia, New Zealand, Ireland, Hungary, and the United States. The World Cancer Research Fund, in conjunction with the Global Cancer Observatory (owned by the International Agency for Research on Cancer), provided a listing of countries with the highest rates of cancer diagnoses per year: with more than three hundred people per 100,000. It is interesting to observe that the countries listed are wealthy in standard per capita macroeconomic terms.

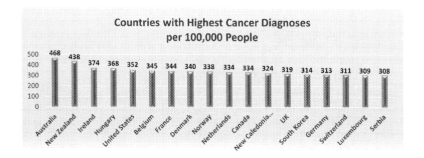

According to the National Cancer Institute (the US National Institutes of Health), in 2020 lung, prostate, and colorectal cancers accounted for an estimated 43 percent of all cancers diagnosed in men in the US. In women, the three most common cancers were breast, lung, and colorectal, which accounted for an estimated 50 percent of all new cancers in the same year. Based on statistics provided by the National Cancer Institute, in 2020 an estimated 1,806,590 new cases of cancer were diagnosed in the US and 606,520 people passed away due to variations of the disease. That was certainly unwelcomed news. The good news is that through January 2019, an estimated 16.9 million people were cancer survivors in the US. The number of cancer survivors is estimated to increase to 22.2 million by 2030.

One of the best books I have read on cancer treatment and survivorship is *A Cancer Survivor's Almanac* by Barbara Hoffman from the National Coalition for Cancer Survivorship. The author provides candid details of the phases and types of cancer treatment. The word *cure* takes on relative meaning for some who must have ongoing treatment and live with the disease all their lives. Her description of the "curative intent treatment" caught my immediate attention. She wrote,

> Cure, from the medical point of view, means that all of the cancer can be removed successfully, or completely eliminated from the body through the use of medications or radiation treatments. Cure also

implies that the likelihood of the cancer returning at a later date—either in the same local area or somewhere else—is extremely low. Curative intent treatment means that the initial treatment plan is chosen with the expectation that the patient will be cured. Although some people have focused on five years of disease-free survival as the equivalent of cure, others may have a very high likelihood of long-term cure after as few as two years of treatment. On the other hand, some may be at risk for recurrent cancer for much longer than five years. Today, curative intent treatment is a realistic goal for many newly diagnosed cancer patients.

There are some types of cancer or stages of cancer where a "cure" may not be a possibility (at least not in the short term), but it nevertheless can be managed to allow a person to have a chance at longevity despite the prevalent reality. Long-term control is a cancer treatment goal aimed at changing the course of the resistant disease, usually by temporarily eliminating the cancer, slowing its growth, and controlling its symptoms. Chronic leukemia, myeloma, and some non-Hodgkin lymphomas often fit this category of cancers that require long-term control.

Beyond the more traditional types of molecularly targeted therapies, such as surgery, chemotherapy, and radiation therapy, hormonal therapies have arisen in the fight against prostate cancer for men by reducing testosterone levels that deprive the cancer cells of this hormone. Similarly, medicines are continuing to be developed to oppose the effects of estrogen on the growth of breast cancer for women. The opportunities for investors to seek out lucrative outcomes in the areas of adjuvant therapy (to treat cancers not usually detected by traditional tests) and neoadjuvant therapy (chemotherapy or hormone therapy used to shrink tumors before the cancer can be removed) are vast and growing with each passing year. As a leukemia patient many years ago, my treatment needed extremely aggressive and extensive usage of intravenous chemotherapy, full-body radiation, and bone marrow transplantation. Today, with advanced technologies available to patients, there are other alternative treatments in lieu of having to endure these crude, invasive treatments. As a result, investors have a much broader array of avenues through which to distribute their funds for profitable opportunities.

It's personal, and it's business.

CHAPTER THREE

Put Your Money Where Your Anger Is

Have the courage of your knowledge and experience. If you have formed a conclusion from the facts and if you know your judgment is sound, act on it—even though others may hesitate or differ. You are neither right nor wrong because the crowd disagrees with you. You are right because your data and reasoning are right. Similarly, in the world of securities, courage becomes the supreme virtue after adequate knowledge and a tested judgement are at hand.
—Benjamin Graham, British-born American investor, economist, and professor widely known as the "father of value investing" and mentor to Warren Buffett

Worldwide, one in six deaths is due to cancer. According to the World Health Organization (WHO) in 2018, approximately 70 percent of deaths from cancer occur in low- and middle-income countries. Tobacco consumption is one of the most important risk factors for cancer and is responsible for 22 percent of cancer deaths in 2018, per the WHO records.

Companies dedicated to fighting cancer and bolstering the immune system are making a significant difference for millions of current and future cancer patients and have produced wonderful financial returns for many investment portfolios. The demand for and supply of new techniques in the fight against cancer are rising as prevalence increases and the world's middle classes increase, particularly those with more readily available access to healthcare and health insurance. One such approach is cancer immunotherapy, which is segmented into the following four key components:

- **technology type** (monoclonal antibodies, cytokines, immunomodulators, and others)
- **application** (lung cancer, breast cancer, colorectal cancer, melanoma, prostate cancer, head and neck cancer, and others)
- **end user** (hospitals, cancer research centers, and clinics)
- **region** (North America, Europe, Asia-Pacific, Latin America, Middle East, and Asia)

Cancer immunotherapy is a treatment that enhances the immune system's ability toward cancer-specific targets and triggering a response capable of destroying cancer cells. Immunotherapy harnesses the power of the body's natural immune system to fight cancer using antibodies engineered to help it recognize camouflaged cancer cells and destroy them. This therapy is preferable to the old, more direct, intrusive techniques because it provides long-term cancer protection, has fewer side effects, and treats a wider range of cancers. Cancer immunotherapy is applied in several types of cancers, such as melanoma, prostate cancer, breast cancer, colorectal cancer, lung cancer, and head and neck cancer. Scientific progress around manipulating genes and cells has been remarkable, along with the pipeline of oncology drugs in clinical development. Although immunotherapy can have side effects, it is nevertheless a huge step up from chemotherapy, which is historically well known for destroying healthy cells along with cancer cells.

Major investment banks such as Goldman Sachs see valuations in the immunotherapy market in the hundreds of billions of dollars, with virtually unlimited upside. As a result, there are steadily growing opportunities for investors to make profits in the oncology and healthcare sectors while making a true difference in the lives of millions of people around the world in the long run. According to Allied Market Research (https://www.alliedmarketresearch.com/cancer-immunotherapy-market), the global cancer immunotherapy market size was valued at approximately $86 billion in 2020 and is projected to reach $310 billion by 2030, registering a compound annual growth rate (CAGR) of 14.1 percent from 2021 to 2030. The key players, among others (as of the publication date of this book), operating in the global cancer immunotherapy market include Amgen, Inc., AstraZeneca, Bayer AG, Bristol-Myers Squibb, Eli Lilly and Company, F. Hoffmann-La Roche, Ltd. (Genentech, Inc.), Pfizer, Inc., Johnson & Johnson (Janssen Global Services, LLC), Merck KGAA, Novartis AG, and a growing number of smaller firms entering the market each year with new and innovative clinical trials.

In contrast, the more traditional (yet still effective) intrusive cancer-fighting approaches entail the global cancer radiation/chemotherapy market. This market is segmented based on the following five categories:

➢ **indication** (lung cancer, breast cancer, colorectal cancer, prostate cancer, stomach cancer, lymphoma, leukemia, ovarian cancer, and others)

➢ **drug class** (alkylating agents, mitotic inhibitors, antimetabolites, topoisomerase inhibitors, antitumor antibiotic, and others)

➢ **route of administration** (intravenous, oral, subcutaneous, intramuscular, intravesicular, topical, intraperitoneal, intraventricular/intrathecal, and others)

➢ **end user** (specialty centers, hospitals, clinics, and others, including ambulatory surgical centers)

> ➤ **geography** (North America held the major share in terms of revenue in the global cancer chemotherapy market, and the region shows the fastest growth over the forecast period from 2020 to 2027; some of the major players in the region include Johnson & Johnson, Eli Lilly, Pfizer, Merck, and Bristol-Myers Squibb.)

The cancer chemotherapy market is expected to grow at a CAGR of around 11.4 percent from 2020 to 2027 and reach the market value of over US$ 74.3 billion by 2027. According to Acumen Research and Consulting, the rising prevalence of cancer worldwide is primarily driving the market growth. In 2019, North America held the major share (percentage) in terms of revenue in the global cancer chemotherapy market, and the region is also anticipated to exhibit the fastest growth over the forecast period from 2020 to 2027. The presence of some of the major players in the region, including Johnson & Johnson, Eli Lilly, Pfizer, Merck, and Bristol-Myers Squibb Company, is further supporting the regional market value.

In the following section, I have included a robust listing of publicly traded cancer-fighting companies for you to consider in building your investment portfolio. I have grouped the companies into five subsections based on the market capitalization ("cap") (stock price multiplied by the number stock shares outstanding).

Market Capitalization	
Micro Cap	Up to $300 Million (Generally Highest Stock Price Volatility)
Small Cap	Greater than $300 Million, up to $2 Billion
Mid Cap	Greater than $2 Billion, up to $10 Billion
Large Cap	Greater than $10 Billion, up to $200 Billion
Mega Cap	Greater than $200 Billion (Generally Lowest Stock Price Volatility)

The information presented below (provided in alphabetical order in each market cap subsection) comes primarily from general descriptions from web sites such as Yahoo! Finance and/or from the respective company's web sites. Please note that at the time of reading this book, some of the companies listed below may no longer exist as distinct, stand-alone operating companies due to being acquired by other firms. Also, you will notice that at the time of publishing this book, the Covid-19 pandemic had wreaked havoc on many of these (particularly smaller) companies due to lost revenues and stymied research and development plans. Nevertheless, this period represents for the long-term investor an excellent (perhaps a once in a lifetime) opportunity to buy "cheap" stocks and enjoy long-term capital appreciation as the global economy returns to some sense of normalcy following this unparalleled time in human history. Remember, as I stated earlier, the global cancer immunotherapy market size was valued at approximately $86 billion in 2020 and is projected to reach $310 billion by 2030, registering a CAGR of 14.1 percent from 2021 to 2030. Likewise, the more traditional cancer chemotherapy/radiation market is expected to grow at a CAGR of around 11.4 percent from 2020 to 2027 and reach market value of over US$ 74.3 billion by 2027.

As a result of these massive shifts in the microeconomics and financial plans for many companies, the winds of mergers and acquisitions (M&A) are blowing with increased speed and intensity. This also produces unique investing opportunities to generate profits from such market shifts. In chapter 7, I will speak briefly about M&A activities and how investors could potentially benefit financially in the biotech industry.

Micro Cap Companies

(Up to $300 Million; Generally Highest Stock Price Volatility)

Aeglea BioTherapeutics (http://ir.aegleabio.com/), whose stock ticker is AGLE, trades on NasdaqGM (Global Market) and is headquartered in Austin, Texas. They are a clinical-stage biotechnology company that designs and develops human enzyme therapeutics for the treatment of rare genetic diseases and cancer, particularly small cell lung cancer. The company's lead product candidate includes a recombinant human arginase 1 enzyme that is in early clinical development stage for the treatment of arginase 1 deficiency, an autosomal recessive metabolic disease caused by a marked decrease in the activity of the native arginase 1 enzyme, and for treating Arginine-dependent cancers. Over a five-year period, the company's stock price fluctuated between the low of $0.51/share and the high of $10.50/share.

Alaunos Therapeutics Inc. (formerly ZIOPHARM Oncology Inc.) (https://ir.alaunos.com/), whose stock ticker is TCRT, trades on NasdaqGS (Global Select) and is headquartered in Houston, Texas. The clinical-stage oncology-focused cell therapy company develops adoptive TCR engineered T-cell therapies. It develops TCR Library that is in phase 1/2 clinical trial for ten TCRs reactive to mutated KRAS, TP53, and EGFR from its TCR library for the treatment of nonsmall cell lung, colorectal, endometrial, pancreatic, ovarian, and bile duct cancers; hunTR, a human neoantigen T-cell receptor platform; and mbIL-15 to treat solid tumors. Alaunos Therapeutics, Inc. has a license agreement with PGEN Therapeutics, Inc.; research and development agreement with the University of Texas MD Anderson Cancer Center; and a patent license agreement and research and development agreement with the National Cancer Institute. The company was founded in 2007. The company was formerly known as ZIOPHARM Oncology, Inc. and changed its name to Alaunos Therapeutics, Inc. in January 2022. Over a

five-year period, the company's stock price fluctuated between the low of $0.52/share and the high of $6.49/share.

Atossa Genetics, Inc. (https://www.atossagenetics.com/investors/), whose stock ticker is ATOS, trades on NasdaqGS (Global Select) and is based in Seattle, Washington. The company develops and markets medical devices, laboratory tests, and therapeutics to address breast health conditions in the United States. Their lead program is the development of an active metabolite of tamoxifen to treat and prevent breast cancer. The company is also developing an intraductal microcatheter technology to potentially target the delivery of therapies, including fulvestrant, immunotherapies, and chimeric antigen receptor T-cell therapies, directly to the site of breast cancer. Their medical devices collect specimens of nipple aspirate fluid for cytological testing. Over a five-year period, the company's stock price fluctuated between the low of $0.81/share and the high of $8.62/share.

AVEO Pharmaceuticals, Inc. (https://investor.aveooncology.com/), whose stock ticker is AVEO, trades on NasdaqGS (Global Select) and is based in Cambridge, Massachusetts. They are a biopharmaceutical company that develops and commercializes a portfolio of targeted medicines for oncology. It markets an oral, once-daily, vascular endothelial growth factor receptor tyrosine kinase inhibitor that is used for the treatment of renal cell carcinoma (RCC). The company is developing potent hepatocyte growth factor inhibitory antibodies for the treatment of squamous cell carcinoma of the head and neck, metastatic pancreatic ductal cancer, acute myeloid leukemia, and esophageal cancer. Over a five-year period, the company's stock price fluctuated between the low of $2.62/share and the high of $33.10/share.

Ayala Pharmaceuticals, Inc. (https://ir.ayalapharma.com/), whose stock ticker is AYLA, trades on NasdaqGM (Global Market) and is headquartered in Rehovot, Israel. They are a clinical-stage biopharmaceutical company that focuses on developing and commercializing small molecule therapeutics for patients suffering from rare and aggressive cancers. The company's lead product candidate is an intravenous, injectable, small molecule gamma secretase inhibitor (GSI) that is in phase 2 clinical trial for the treatment of recurrent/metastatic adenoid cystic carcinoma for patients bearing Notch-activating mutations. It is also involved in developing an oral, injectable, small molecule GSI that is in phase 1 clinical trial for the treatment of desmoid tumors. Ayala Pharmaceuticals, Inc. has a collaboration agreement with Novartis International Pharmaceutical Limited to develop AL102 for the treatment of multiple myeloma. Over a five-year period, the company's stock price fluctuated between the low of $0.63/share and the high of $21.00/share.

Bellicum Pharmaceuticals, Inc. (http://ir.bellicum.com/), whose stock ticker is BLCM, trades on NasdaqGS (Global Select) and is based in Houston, Texas. They are a clinical-stage biopharmaceutical company that focuses on discovering and developing novel cellular immunotherapies for the treatment of hematological cancers, solid tumors, and orphan inherited blood disorders in the United States and other countries. The company's clinical product candidates include clinical trials to improve hematopoietic stem cell transplantation outcomes in the treatment of hematologic malignancies, including leukemia, lymphoma, and inherited blood disorders. Over a five-year period, the company's stock price fluctuated between the low of $1.01/share and the high of $103.80/share.

Beyond Spring, Inc. (https://ir.beyondspringpharma.com/stock-information/stock-quote), whose stock ticker is BYSI, trades on NasdaqCM (Capital Market) and is based in New York, New York. It is a clinical-stage biopharmaceutical company that focuses on the development and commercialization of immuno-oncology cancer therapies. The company's lead asset is an anticancer agent in combination with docetaxel in advanced nonsmall cell lung cancer (NSCLC) for the prevention of high and intermediate risk chemotherapy-induced neutropenia. It is also developing antibodies to treat small cell lung cancer. Over a five-year period, the company's stock price fluctuated between the low of $0.81/share and the high of $36.28/share.

BriaCell Therapeutics Corp. (https://investors.briacell. com/), whose stock ticker is BCTX, trades on NasdaqCM (Capital Market) and is headquartered in West Vancouver, Canada. They are an immuno-oncology biotechnology company that engages in developing immunotherapies for the treatment of cancer. In August 2021, the company announced a collaboration with ImaginAb, a market-leading global biotechnology company to evaluate immunotherapy imaging technology in advanced breast cancer. Their lead candidate is Bria-IMT, which is in phase 1/2A clinical trial in a combination study with immune checkpoint inhibitors for the treatment of breast cancer. The company also has a cooperative research and development agreement with the National Cancer Institute for developing Bria-OTS, a personalized immunotherapy for advanced breast cancer, and BriaDx, a diagnostic test. Over a five-year period, the company's stock price fluctuated between the low of $6.21/share and the high of $42.00/share.

Calithera Biosciences, Inc. (http://ir.calithera.com/stock-information/stock-quote), whose stock ticker is CALA, trades on NasdaqGS (Global Select) and is based in San Francisco, California. It is a clinical-stage biopharmaceutical company that focuses on the discovery and development of small molecule drugs directed against tumor metabolism and tumor immunology targets for the treatment of cancer in the United States. Their lead product candidate is an inhibitor of glutaminase that is in phase 2 clinical trial to treat solid tumors. The company also offers an oral inhibitor of arginase that is in phase 1/2 clinical trial for the treatment of hematology and oncology. Over a five-year period, the company's stock price fluctuated between the low of $2.46/share and the high of $344/share.

Cardiff Oncology, Inc. (https://cardiffoncology.investorroom. com/), whose stock ticker is CRDF, trades on NasdaqCM (Capital

Market) and is headquartered in San Diego, California. It is a clinical-stage biotechnology company with the singular mission of developing new treatment options for cancer patients in indications with the greatest medical need. The company primarily serves pharmaceutical companies. Their lead drug candidate is a selective adenosine triphosphate competitive inhibitor that is in phase 1B/2 clinical trial in acute myeloid leukemia (AML) and has completed a phase 1 clinical trial in advanced solid tumors and phase 1B/2 clinical trial for metastatic colorectal cancer in combination with FOLFIRI and Avastin. The company's onvansertib is also in phase 2 clinical trial in combination with Zytiga for metastatic castration-resistant prostate cancer. In addition, it develops therapeutics, such as belinostat (Beleodaq), quizartinib (AC220), a development stage FLT3 inhibitor, and bortezomib (Velcade) for the treatment of leukemias, lymphomas, and solid tumor cancers. Over a five-year period, the company's stock price fluctuated between the low of $0.97/share and the high of $53.28/share.

CASI Pharmaceuticals, Inc. (https://www.casipharmaceuticals. com/investor-relations/), whose stock ticker is CASI, trades on NasdaqGS (Global Select) and is based in Rockville, Maryland. The pharmaceutical company develops products and various therapeutics in China, the United States, and other countries. The company's product pipeline includes a melphalan hydrochloride for injection primarily for use as a high-dose conditioning treatment prior to hematopoietic progenitor cell transplantation in patients with multiple myeloma. Their product pipeline also comprises an ibritumomab tiuxetan injection for intravenous treatment of patients with relapsed or refractory, low-grade, or follicular B-cell non-Hodgkin lymphoma, as well as for the treatment of patients with previously untreated follicular non-Hodgkin lymphoma, and a microtubule inhibitor to treat adult patients with Philadelphia chromosome-negative acute lymphoblastic leukemia. Over a five-year period, the company's stock price fluctuated between the low of $2.04/share and the high of $82.30/share.

Cellectar Biosciences, Inc. (https://investor.cellectar.com/), whose stock ticker is CLRB, trades on NasdaqGS (Global Select) and is based in Florham Park, New Jersey. They are a clinical-stage biopharmaceutical company that focuses on the discovery, development, and commercialization of drugs for the treatment of cancer. Their lead phospholipid drug conjugate (PDC) candidate is in phase 2 clinical study in patients with relapsed or refractory (R/R) multiple myeloma (MM) and a range of B-cell malignancies, as well as in phase 1 clinical study for R/R MM. The company also develops a chemotherapeutic program that is targeted to treat solid tumors. Over a five-year period, the company's stock price fluctuated between the low of $1.82/share and the high of $153.00/share.

Champions Oncology, Inc. (https://championsoncology.com/investors/stock-information/), whose stock ticker is CSBR, trades on NasdaqGS (Global Select) and is based in Hackensack, New Jersey. The company develops and sells technology solutions and products to personalize the development and use of oncology drugs in the United States. The company, through their platform, provides Personalized Oncology Solutions (POS) that assist physicians in developing personalized treatment options for cancer patients through tumor specific data obtained from drug panels and related personalized oncology services. Over a five-year period, the company's stock price fluctuated between the low of $3.25/share and the high of $17.47/share.

Clovis Oncology, Inc. (https://ir.clovisoncology.com/investors-and-news/default.aspx), whose stock ticker is CLVS, trades on NasdaqGS (Global Select) and is based in Boulder, Colorado. The biopharmaceutical company focuses on acquiring, developing, and commercializing anticancer agents in the United States, the European Union, and elsewhere. The company offers an oral, small molecule inhibitor of poly ADP-ribose polymerase for recurrent epithelial ovarian, fallopian tube, or primary peritoneal cancer. The company distributes their products primarily through specialty distributors and pharmacy providers to patients and healthcare providers. Over a five-year period, the company's stock price fluctuated between the low of $0.69/share and the high of $76.99/share.

CTI BioPharma Corp. (https://investors.ctibiopharma.com/), whose stock ticker is CTIC, trades on NasdaqCM (Capital Market) and is headquartered in Seattle, Washington. The biopharmaceutical company focuses on the acquisition, development, and commercialization of novel targeted therapies for blood-related cancers in the United States and other countries. It develops a novel aza-anthracenedione for the treatment of adult patients with multiply relapsed or refractory aggressive B-cell non-Hodgkin lymphoma and an investigational oral kinase inhibitor. Over a five-year period, the company's stock price fluctuated between the low of $0.69/share and the high of $7.43/share.

Epizyme, Inc. (https://epizyme.gcs-web.com/), whose stock ticker is EPZM, trades on NasdaqGS (Global Select). They are a late-stage biopharmaceutical company based in Cambridge, Massachusetts, that discovers, develops, and commercializes novel epigenetic medicines for patients with cancer and other diseases primarily in the United States. The company's lead products candidate is an inhibitor of the EZH2 histone methyltransferase that is in the phase 2 clinical trial for patients with relapsed or refractory non-Hodgkin lymphoma (NHL). The company develops clinical trials for relapsed or refractory patients with mesothelioma characterized by BAP1 loss of function and for children with epithelioid sarcoma and other INI1-negative solid tumors. The company is completing studies in the treatment of acute myeloid leukemia and acute lymphoblastic leukemia. Over a five-year period, the company's stock price fluctuated between the low of $0.40/share and the high of $28.00/share.

Fennec Pharmaceuticals Inc. (https://investors.fennecpharma.com/), whose stock ticker is FENC, trades on NasdaqGS (Global Select) and is based in Research Triangle Park, North Carolina. The biopharmaceutical company develops product candidates for use in the treatment of various cancers in the United States. Their lead product is PEDMARK, a formulation of sodium thiosulfate that has completed the phase 3 clinical trial for the prevention of cisplatin-induced hearing loss or ototoxicity in children. The company was formerly known as Adherex Technologies Inc. and changed its name to Fennec Pharmaceuticals Inc. in September 2014. Fennec Pharmaceuticals Inc. was founded in 1996. Over a five-year period, the company's stock price fluctuated between the low of $1.58/share and the high of $8.75/share.

Fortress Biotech, Inc. (https://www.fortressbiotech.com/investors), whose stock ticker is FBIO, trades on NasdaqGS (Global Select) and is based in New York, New York. The company is a combination of ten companies with more than twenty products in their pipeline. The company has a variety of drugs for indications, such as glioblastoma, acute myeloid leukemia, metastatic breast cancer, and other cancer varieties. The company has developed a gene therapy for X-linked severe combined immunodeficiency, a clinical trial to reduce amyloid deposits in the tissues and organs, a chimeric antigen receptor engineered T-cell (CAR T) program for acute myeloid leukemia, a program for B cell non-Hodgkin lymphoma, and a program for multiple myeloma and light chain amyloidosis. In addition, it develops products for glioblastoma (GBM) breast cancer and brain metastases, prostate and pancreatic cancers, nonsmall cell lung cancer, and metastatic cancer. Over a five-year period, the company's stock price fluctuated between the low of $0.49/share and the high of $6.27/share.

Genocea Biosciences, Inc. (https://ir.genocea.com/), whose stock ticker is GNCA, trades on NasdaqCM (Capital Market) and is based in Cambridge, Massachusetts. The biopharmaceutical company discovers and develops cancer immunotherapies. The company uses their proprietary discovery platform to recall a patient's preexisting T cell immune responses to tumors to identify neoantigens and antigens for inclusion in vaccines that are designed to act through T cell (or cellular) immune responses. Their lead immuno-oncology program is an adjuvanted neoantigen peptide vaccine candidate that is in clinical trial, designed to direct a patient's immune system to attack tumors. Over a five-year period, the company's stock price fluctuated between the low of $0.13/share and the high of $11.29/share.

Infinity Pharmaceuticals, Inc. (http://investors.infi.com/), whose stock ticker is INFI, trades on NasdaqGS (Global Select) and is based in Cambridge, Massachusetts. The biopharmaceutical company develops medicines for people with cancer in the United States. Their product candidate is an orally administered clinical-stage immuno-oncology product candidate that inhibits the enzyme phosphoinositide-3-kinase-gamma (PI3K-gamma) that is in phase 1/1B clinical study. The company has strategic alliances with other companies to complete clinical trials for patients with relapsed or refractory chronic lymphocytic leukemia or small lymphocytic lymphoma. Over a five-year period, the company's stock price fluctuated between the low of $0.49/share and the high of $6.12/share.

Loncar Cancer Immunotherapy ETF (Exchange-Traded Fund) (https://loncarfunds.com), whose stock ticker is CNCR, trades on NasdaqGM (Global Market). The fund seeks to track the total return performance of the Loncar Cancer Immunotherapy Index. The index is composed of the common stock of approximately thirty pharmaceutical or biotechnology companies having a high strategic focus on the development of drugs that harness the body's own immune system to fight cancer. Over a five-year period, the ETF price fluctuated between the low of $12.00/share and the high of $36.12/share.

NantHealth, Inc. (https://ir.nanthealth.com/), whose stock ticker is NH, trades on NasdaqGS (Global Select) and is headquartered in Culver City, California. Together with its subsidiaries, the healthcare technology company operates in the United States and other countries. The company engages in converging science and technology through an integrated clinical platform to provide health information at the point of care that integrates patient data management, bioinformatics, and molecular medicine to enable value-based care and evidence-based clinical practice. The company's products include GPS Cancer, a molecular profile that integrates whole genome sequencing of tumor and normal germline samples, as well as whole transcriptome sequencing, GPS Cancer Report, a GPS cancer solution, Liquid GPS, a blood-based molecular test, and Eviti, a decision support solution. Over a five-year period, the company's stock price fluctuated between the low of $0.25/share and the high of $6.56/share.

Navidea Biopharmaceuticals (https://ir.navidea.com/), whose stock ticker is NAVB, trades on the New York Stock Exchange (NYSE) and is headquartered in Dublin, Ohio. The biopharmaceutical company focuses on the development and commercialization of precision immunodiagnostic agents and immunotherapeutics. Navidea seeks to develop next-generation targeted diagnostics and therapies for cancer, autoimmune conditions, and other inflammatory diseases. Their CD206-targeted drug platform is applicable to a range of diagnostic modalities, including single photon emission computed tomography, positron emission tomography (PET), imaging and topical gamma scanning, and intra-operative and/or optical-fluorescence detection, as well as delivery of therapeutic compounds that target macrophages, and immune-and inflammation-involved diseases. Over a five-year period, the company's stock price fluctuated between the low of $0.25/share and the high of $9.35/share.

OncoCyte Corporation (https://investors.oncocyte.com/), whose stock ticker is OCX, trades on NYSE and is headquartered in Irvine, California. The company engages in the development and commercialization of proprietary laboratory-developed tests for the detection of cancer. They offer molecular tests for early-stage adenocarcinoma of the lung and novel gene expression-based tests. It also develops non-invasive blood-based tests used to detect lung cancer. OncoCyte Corporation has a strategic collaboration with Guardian Research Network, Inc. to create a solution for pharma clients from patient recruitment to regulatory approvals. The company was founded in 2009. Over a five-year period, the company's stock price fluctuated between the low of $0.76/share and the high of $7.00/share.

Oncolytics Biotech, Inc. (https://ir.oncolyticsbiotech.com/), whose stock ticker is ONCY, trades on NasdaqCM (Capital Market) and is headquartered in Calgary, Canada. The development stage biopharmaceutical company focuses on the discovery and development of pharmaceutical products for the treatment of cancer. Their lead product is an immuno-oncology viral agent for the treatment of solid tumors and hematological malignancies. The company has an agreement with Merck and Pfizer to codevelop pelareorep in combination with paclitaxel and avelumab, a human anti-PD-L1 antibody for the treatment of hormone-receptor positive, human epidermal growth factor 2-negative metastatic breast cancer. Over a five-year period, the company's stock price fluctuated between the low of $0.50/share and the high of $8.50/share.

Organovo Holdings, Inc. (https://ir.organovo.com/investor-overview), whose stock ticker is ONVO, trades on NasdaqGS (Global Select) and is headquartered in San Diego, California. The biotechnology company develops bioprinted human tissues based on their 3D human tissue platform technology that emulate human biology and diseases. Their 3D human tissue platform includes their proprietary bioprinters that are automated devices that enable the fabrication of 3D living tissues comprised mammalian cells and related technologies for preparing bioinks and bioprinting multicellular tissues with complex architecture. Over a five-year period, the company's stock price fluctuated between the low of $1.71/share and the high of $42.00/share.

PDS Biotechnology Corporation (https://www.pdsbiotech.com/investors/investor-resources/corporate-presentations), whose stock ticker is PDSB, trades on NasdaqCM (Capital Market) and is based in Florham Park, New Jersey. The clinical-stage biopharmaceutical company focuses on developing multifunctional cancer immunotherapies. Their lead product candidate is in phase 2 clinical trial that provides a first line treatment for the recurrent/ metastatic head and neck cancer, human papillomavirus associated malignancies, and cervical cancer. The company is also developing various product candidates that are in preclinical trials, including PDS0102 T-cell receptor gamma alternate reading frame protein (TARP) for treating prostate and breast cancers; PDS0103 (MUC-1) for ovarian, colorectal, lung, and breast cancers; and PDS0104, which includes tyrosinase-related protein 2 for the treatment of melanoma. The company has a license and collaboration agreements with National Institutes of Health, Merck Eprova AG, the US Department of Health and Human Services, and MSD International GmbH. PDS Biotechnology Corporation was founded in 2005. Over a five-year period, the company's stock price fluctuated between the low of $0.67/share and the high of $344.00/share.

Spectrum Pharmaceuticals, Inc. (http://investor.sppirx. com/index.php/), whose stock ticker is SPPI, trades on NasdaqGS (Global Select) and is headquartered in Henderson, Nevada. The company develops and commercializes oncology and hematology drug products. It offers treatments for peripheral T-cell lymphoma (PTCL), an injection to treat non-Hodgkin lymphoma, and a product for adult patients with Philadelphia chromosome-negative acute lymphoblastic leukemia. The company produces an inhibitor for the treatment of patients with relapsed or refractory PTCL and products for use as a conditioning treatment prior to autologous stem cell transplant in multiple myeloma patients. They are also developing a pan-HER inhibitor for nonsmall cell lung cancer tumors and products for chemotherapy-induced neutropenia and nonmuscle invasive bladder cancer. The company sells their drugs through group purchasing organizations, wholesalers, and directly to hospitals and cancer centers in the United States and through distributors in Europe. Over a five-year period, the company's stock price fluctuated between the low of $0.38/share and the high of $24.53/share.

Surface Oncology, Inc. (https://investors.surfaceoncology.com/), whose stock ticker is SURF, trades on NasdaqGS (Global Select) and is headquartered in Cambridge, Massachusetts. The clinical-stage immuno-oncology company engages in the development of cancer therapies. The company develops human immunoglobulin isotype G4 monoclonal antibodies, including SRF231 inhibiting CD47, NZV930 inhibiting CD73, SRF617 inhibiting CD39, SRF388 targeting interleukin 27, and SRF813 targeting CD112R. It also develops various earlier stage programs that target other critical components of the tumor microenvironment, including regulatory T cells and natural killer cells. The company has a strategic collaboration agreement with Novartis Institutes for Biomedical Research, Inc. for the development of cancer therapies, the Merck Sharp & Dohme Corp. to evaluate the safety and efficacy of combining Surface's SRF617, an investigational antibody therapy targeting CD39, and Merck's KEYTRUDAÃ (pembrolizumab), the first anti-PD-1 therapy approved in the United States. Over a five-year period, the company's stock price fluctuated between the low of $0.99/share and the high of $17.01/share.

Synlogic, Inc. (https://investor.synlogictx.com/), whose stock ticker is SYBX, trades on NasdaqGS (Global Select) and is headquartered in Cambridge, Massachusetts. The clinical-stage biopharmaceutical company focuses on the discovery and development of synthetic biotic medicines to treat metabolic, inflammatory, and cancer diseases in the United States. Their lead therapeutic programs include an oral therapy for the treatment of an excess of ammonia in the blood, which includes patients with liver diseases such as hepatic encephalopathy, as well as patients with urea cycle disorders. The company is also developing an intratumorally administered synthetic biotic medicine to treat immuno-oncology solid tumors. Over a five-year period, the company's stock price fluctuated between the low of $1.06/share and the high of $14.21/share.

Syros Pharmaceuticals, Inc. (https://ir.syros.com/), whose stock ticker is SYRS, trades on NasdaqGS (Global Select) and is headquartered in Cambridge, Massachusetts. The biopharmaceutical company focuses on developing treatments for cancer and monogenic diseases and is building a pipeline of gene control medicines. Their lead product candidates include a selective retinoic acid receptor alpha agonist, which is in clinical trial for genomically defined subsets of patients with acute myeloid leukemia (AML) and myelodysplastic syndrome, a selective cyclin-dependent kinase 7 (CDK7) inhibitor, which is in clinical trial that is used for treating patients with solid tumors and blood cancers, including ovarian and breast cancer, and a CDK7 inhibitor, which is in preclinical studies to treat oncology patients. Over a five-year period, the company's stock price fluctuated between the low of $4.44/share and the high of $144.70/share.

Tracon Pharmaceuticals (https://traconpharma.gcs-web.com/), whose stock ticker is TCON, trades on NasdaqGM (Global Market) and is based in San Diego, California. The clinical-stage biopharmaceutical company focuses on the development and commercialization of novel targeted therapeutics for cancer, age-related macular degeneration, and fibrotic diseases. They are a leader in the field of endoglin biology and are using their expertise to develop antibodies that bind to the endoglin receptor. Their lead product candidate is an anti-endoglin antibody that is being developed for the treatment of multiple solid tumor types in combination with inhibitors of the VEGF pathway. Their other product candidates are an anti-endoglin antibody that is in preclinical development for the treatment of fibrotic diseases and a small molecule that is in clinical development for the treatment of lung cancer and glioblastoma. Each of their product candidates is expected to complement currently available therapies. Over a five-year period, the company's stock price fluctuated between the low of $1.09/share and the high of $33.50/share.

Viracta Therapeutics, Inc. (https://viracta.investorroom.com/), whose stock ticker is VIRX, trades on NasdaqGS (Global

Select) and is headquartered in Cardiff-by-the-Sea, California. The precision oncology company engages in developing drugs for the treatment of virus-associated malignancies. The company's proprietary investigational drug, nanatinostat, is currently being evaluated in combination with the antiviral agent valganciclovir as an oral combination therapy in a phase 2 clinical trial for EBV-positive lymphomas. Viracta is pursuing application of this inducible synthetic lethality approach in other EBV-associated malignancies, such as nasopharyngeal carcinoma, gastric carcinoma, and other virus-related cancers. Over a five-year period, the company's stock price fluctuated between the low of $1.87/share and the high of $245.61/share.

Small Cap Companies
(Greater than $300 Million, up to $2 Billion)

Adaptimmune PLC (https://ir.adaptimmune.com/), whose stock ticker is ADAP, trades on NasdaqGS (Global Select). The company is based in Abingdon, UK, and is a clinical-stage biopharmaceutical company that focuses on providing novel cell therapies primarily to US patients with solid tumors. The company's specific peptide enhanced affinity receptor T-cell platform enables it to identify cancer targets. It is involved in developing clinical trials for the treatment of nonsmall cell lung cancer (NSCLC), as well as urothelial, melanoma, and head and neck cancers. The company is focusing on clinical trials for solid tumor indication that include urothelial, melanoma, head and neck, ovarian, NSCLC, esophageal, gastric, synovial sarcoma, and myxoid round cell liposarcoma cancers as well as hepatocellular carcinoma. Over a five-year period, the company's stock price fluctuated between the low of $0.73/share and the high of $13.90/share.

    Agenus Inc. (https://investor.agenusbio.com/contacts), whose stock ticker is AGEN, trades on NasdaqCM (Capital Market) and is based in Lexington, Massachusetts. They are a clinical-stage immuno-oncology company that focuses on the discovery and development of therapies that engage the body's immune system to fight cancer. The company offers an antibody discovery platform for the identification of fully human and humanized monoclonal antibodies and an antibody discovery platform used for the generation of novel monoclonal antibodies. In addition, the company develops vaccine programs designed to induce immunity against a class of tumors and a host of other antibodies that are under various stages of development. Over a five-year period, the company's stock price fluctuated between the low of $1.57/share and the high of $6.50/share.

Agios Pharmaceuticals, Inc. (https://investor.agios.com/investor-overview), whose stock ticker is AGIO, trades on NasdaqGS (Global Select) and is based in Cambridge, Massachusetts. They are a biopharmaceutical company that engages in the discovery and development of medicines in the field of cellular metabolism and adjacent areas of biology for the treatment of cancer and rare genetic diseases. The company offers an oral targeted inhibitor for treating adult patients with relapsed or refractory acute myeloid leukemia (R/R AML), as well as to treat patients with newly diagnosed AML, and an oral targeted inhibitor for patients with R/R AML. It is also developing drugs to treat frontline AML and completing clinical trials for the treatment of bile duct cancer, as well as in early-stage clinical development to treat glioma (a tumor that originates in the glial cells of the brain or spinal cord) and other solid tumors. Over a five-year period, the company's stock price fluctuated between the low of $17.97/share and the high of $97.38/share.

ALX Oncology Holdings Inc. (https://ir.alxoncology.com/), whose stock ticker is ALXO, trades on NasdaqGS (Global Select) and is based in Burlingame, California. It is a clinical-stage immuno-oncology company that focuses on developing therapies for patients fighting cancer. Their lead product candidate is ALX148, a CD47 blocking therapeutic used for the treatment of myelodysplastic syndromes and acute myeloid leukemia, as well as a range of solid tumor indications, including head and neck squamous cell and human epidermal growth factor receptor 2 positive gastric/gastroesophageal junction carcinoma. The company was founded in 2015. Over a five-year period, the company's stock price fluctuated between the low of $6.47/share and the high of $88.64/share.

AngioDynamics, Inc. (https://investors.angiodynamics.com/), whose stock ticker is ANGO, trades on NasdaqGS (Global Select) and is headquartered in Latham, New York. The company designs, manufactures, and sells various medical, surgical, and diagnostic devices used by professional healthcare providers for the treatment of peripheral vascular disease and vascular access and for use in oncology and surgical settings in the United States and other countries. Additionally, the company offers peripherally inserted central catheters, midline catheters, implantable ports, dialysis catheters, and related accessories and supplies that are used primarily to deliver short-term drug therapies, such as chemotherapeutic agents and antibiotics, into the central venous system. They sell and market their products to interventional radiologists, interventional cardiologists, vascular surgeons, urologists, interventional and surgical oncologists, and critical care nurses directly, as well as through distributor relationships. The company was founded in 1988. Over a five-year period, the company's stock price fluctuated between the low of $8.26/share and the high of $30.97/share.

Atara Biotherapeutics, Inc. (http://investors.atarabio.com/), whose stock ticker is ATRA, trades on NasdaqGS (Global Select) and is based in San Francisco, California. They are an off-the-shelf T-cell immunotherapy company that develops treatments for patients with cancer, autoimmune, and viral diseases in the United States. It is developing a T-cell immunotherapy that is phase 3 clinical trials for the treatment of rituximab-refractory Epstein-Barr virus (EBV) associated posttransplant lymphoproliferative disorder, as well as other EBV associated hematologic and solid tumors, including nasopharyngeal carcinoma. The company is also developing next-generation CAR T immunotherapies for patients with hematologic malignancies and solid tumors, and autoimmune and viral diseases, acute myeloid leukemia (AML), and lymphomas. In addition, it is developing drugs against human papillomavirus and associated cancers, tumors, cytomegalovirus, and related diseases. Over a five-year period, the company's stock price fluctuated between the low of $3.22/share and the high of $50.20/share.

Autolus Therapeutics PLC (https://www.autolus.com/investor-relations), whose stock ticker is AUTL, trades on NasdaqGS (Global Select) and is based in London, UK. The biopharmaceutical company develops T cell therapies for the treatment of cancer. The company is developing products for B cell malignancies, the treatment of multiple myeloma, T cell lymphoma, and the treatment of solid tumors. Utilizing their advanced cell programming and manufacturing technologies, Autolus has a pipeline of products in development for the treatment of hematological malignancies. Over a five-year period, the company's stock price fluctuated between the low of $2.04/share and the high of $48.01/share.

Berkeley Lights, Inc. (https://investors.berkeleylights.com), whose stock ticker is BLI, trades on NasdaqGS (Global Select) and is headquartered in Emeryville, California. They are a digital cell biology company that focuses on enabling and accelerating the rapid development and commercialization of biotherapeutics and other cell-based products. Berkeley Lights focuses on cellular therapy, biopharmaceuticals, and genomics. The company has developed a tech platform for the rapid functional characterization of single cells at scale. The company develops and commercializes T cell therapies that have shown to be highly effective in fighting cancerous tumors. The company was incorporated in 2011. Lights went public in July 2020 after launching a successful IPO. Over a five-year period, the company's stock price fluctuated between the low of $1.97/share and the high of $103.38/share.

Bicycle Therapeutics Plc (https://investors.bicycletherapeutics.com/), whose stock ticker is BCYC, trades on NasdaqGS (Global

Select) and is headquartered in Cambridge, UK. It is a clinical-stage biopharmaceutical company that develops a class of medicines for diseases that are underserved by existing therapeutics. Their lead product candidate is a bicycle toxin conjugate (BTC) that is in phase 1/2A clinical trials targeting tumors that express membrane type 1 matrix metalloprotease. The company's oncology product candidates also comprise a BTC that is in a phase 1/2A clinical trial targeting EphA2, BT8009, which is in preclinical studies targeting Nectin-4, and CD137, an immune cell costimulatory molecule that is in preclinical stage. It has a clinical trial and license agreement with the Cancer Research Technology Limited and CRUK; research collaboration agreements with AstraZeneca, Sanofi, Oxurion, and the Dementia Discovery Fund; and discovery collaboration and license agreement with Genentech for the discovery and development of Bicycle peptides for multiple immuno-oncology targets. Bicycle Therapeutics PLC was incorporated in 2009. Over a five-year period, the company's stock price fluctuated between the low of $7.80/share and the high of $60.87/share.

Bluebird Bio Inc. (http://investor.bluebirdbio.com/), whose stock ticker is BLUE, trades on NasdaqGS (Global Select) and is based in Cambridge, Massachusetts. The clinical-stage biotechnology company focuses on developing transformative gene therapies for severe genetic diseases and cancer. The company focuses on product candidates in the treatment of multiple myeloma. It has strategic collaborations with major pharmaceutical companies to discover, develop, and commercialize disease-altering gene therapies in oncology and various immune cell therapies for cancer. Over a five-year period, the company's stock price fluctuated between the low of $3.16/share and the high of $150.23/share.

Burning Rock Biotech Limited (https://www.brbiotech.com/news/details/410), whose stock ticker is BNR, trades on NasdaqGS (Global Select) and is based in Guangzhou, China. The company primarily develops and provides cancer therapy selection tests focusing on therapy selection testing for late-stage cancer patients, especially in the People's Republic of China. The company primarily offers thirteen next-generation sequencing-based cancer therapy selection tests applicable to a range of cancer types, including lung cancer, gastrointestinal cancer, prostate cancer, breast cancer, lymphomas, thyroid cancer, colorectal cancer, ovarian cancer, pancreatic cancer, and bladder cancer using tissue and liquid biopsy samples. Their principal products target therapy and immunotherapy, as well as immunotherapy-related biomarkers, such as microsatellite instability and tumor mutation burden, and NTRK fusions, and LungPlasma, a circulating tumor DNA liquid biopsy-based test for nonsmall cell lung cancer. It also offers testing for gastrointestinal cancers. Burning Rock Biotech Limited has collaborations on clinical trials and research studies with major pharmaceutical companies primarily through central laboratory and companion diagnostics development services to pharmaceutical companies. The company was founded in 2014. Over a five-year period, the company's stock price fluctuated between the low of $2.12/share and the high of $36.81/share.

Cerus Corporation (http://www.cerus.com/Investors/Investor-Overview/default.aspx), whose stock ticker is CERS, trades on NasdaqGS (Global Select) and is based in Concord, California. It is a biomedical products company that focuses on developing and commercializing the enhancement of blood safety. Their system is a proprietary technology for controlling biological replication that is designed to reduce blood-borne pathogens in donated blood components intended for transfusion. The company offers systems designed to inactivate blood-borne pathogens in platelets and plasma donated for transfusion and a system to inactivate blood-borne pathogens in red blood cells donated for transfusion. It markets platelet and plasma systems through their direct sales force and distributors in the United States, Europe, the Commonwealth of Independent States, the Middle East, Latin America, and other regions. Over a five-year period, the company's stock price fluctuated between the low of $2.88/share and the high of $8.07/share.

Cullinan Oncology (https://investors.cullinanoncology.

com/), whose stock ticker is CGEM, trades on NasdaqGS (Global Select) and is headquartered in Cambridge, Massachusetts. The biopharmaceutical company focuses on developing a pipeline of targeted oncology and immuno-oncology therapies for cancer patients in the United States. The company's lead candidate is an orally available small molecule that is in a phase 1/2A dose escalation and expansion trial for treating patients with nonsmall cell lung cancer. Their preclinical products include a humanized bispecific antibody for the treatment of acute myeloid leukemia, a monoclonal antibody for the treatment of solid tumors, a fusion protein for the treatment of solid tumors, a T cell engaging antibody for B-cell malignancies, a bispecific fusion protein to block the PD-1 axis and to activate the 4-IBB/CD137 pathway on T cells in tumors, and a cell therapy to target a novel senescence and cancer-related protein. Cullinan Management, Inc. was incorporated in 2016. Over a five-year period, the company's stock price fluctuated between the low of $9.81/share and the high of $48.06/share.

G1 Therapeutics, Inc. (http://investor.g1therapeutics.com/), whose stock ticker is GTHX, trades on NasdaqGS (Global Select) and is headquartered in Research Triangle Park, North Carolina. The clinical-stage biopharmaceutical company engages in the discovery, development, and commercialization of small molecule therapeutics for the treatment of patients with cancer. It is developing an intravenous cyclin-dependent kinases (CDK) 4/6 inhibitor for patients with extensive-stage small cell lung cancer (SCLC), as well as for patients with first line (SCLC) and metastatic triple-negative breast cancer and nonsmall cell lung cancer. G1 Therapeutics, Inc. has a collaboration with Quantum Leap Healthcare Collaborative to evaluate Trilaciclib for neoadjuvant treatment of locally advanced breast cancer. Over a five-year period, the company's stock price fluctuated between the low of $4.38/share and the high of $67.85/share.

Geron Corporation (https://ir.geron.com/home/default.aspx), whose stock ticker is GERN, trades on NasdaqGS (Global Select) and is based in Menlo Park, California. The clinical biopharmaceutical company focuses on the development and commercialization of therapeutics for hematologic myeloid malignancies. The company supports the clinical-stage development of a telomerase inhibitor for the treatment of hematologic myeloid malignancies. Over a five-year period, the company's stock price fluctuated between the low of $0.96/share and the high of $6.08/share.

Gritstone Bio, Inc. (https://ir.gritstonebio.com/), whose stock ticker is GRTS, trades on NasdaqGS (Global Select) and is headquartered in Emeryville, California. The clinical-stage biotechnology company engages in developing tumor-specific cancer immunotherapies to fight various cancer types and infectious diseases. Their lead product candidate is GRANITE, which is in phase 1/2 clinical trial for the treatment of solid tumors, including metastatic nonsmall cell lung cancer, as well as gastroesophageal, bladder and microsatellite stable, and colorectal cancers. The company is also developing SLATE, an off-the-shelf immunotherapy candidate for the treatment of common solid tumors, including metastatic nonsmall cell lung cancer, colorectal cancer, pancreatic cancer, and other mutation-positive tumors. Gritstone Bio, Inc. was founded in 2015. Over a five-year period, the company's stock price fluctuated between the low of $1.85/share and the high of $27.11/share.

Innate Pharma SA (https://investors.innate-pharma.com/), whose stock ticker is IPHA, trades on NasdaqGS (Global Select) and is headquartered in Marseille, France. The clinical-stage biotechnology company discovers and develops therapeutic antibodies for the treatment of cancer in France and other countries. The company offers in clinical trial an anti-KIR3DL2 humanized cytotoxicity-inducing antibody for cutaneous T-cell lymphomas, an immune checkpoint inhibitor that is in clinical trial to treat various cancer indications and tumors, and a therapeutic antibody that binds and blocks C5a receptors expressed on subsets of myeloid-derived suppressor cells and neutrophils. They also provide an anti-CD39 antibody and an anti-CD73 antibody that is in preclinical stage for the treatment of immuno-oncology. In addition, the company offers a bispecific NK cell engager that is used to create novel molecular formats to kill tumor cells. Furthermore, it provides a commercial-stage oncology product for treating hairy cell leukemia. Over a five-year period, the company's stock price fluctuated between the low of $2.00/share and the high of $8.10/share.

Inovio Pharmaceuticals, Inc. (http://ir.inovio.com/investors/default.aspx), whose stock ticker is INO, trades on NasdaqGS (Global Select) and is based in Plymouth Meeting, Pennsylvania. The late-stage biotechnology company focuses on the discovery, development, and commercialization of DNA-based immunotherapies and vaccines to prevent and treat cancers and infectious diseases. Their SynCon immunotherapy design can break the immune system's tolerance of cancerous cells and is intended to facilitate cross-strain protection against known as well as new, unmatched strains of pathogens such as influenza. The company is involved in conducting and planning clinical studies of their proprietary immunotherapies for human papillomavirus-caused precancers and cancers and glioblastoma. Over a five-year period, the company's stock price fluctuated between the low of $1.51/share and the high of $29.98/share.

Kura Oncology, Inc. (https://ir.kuraoncology.com/), whose stock ticker is KURA, trades on NasdaqGS (Global Select) and is headquartered in San Diego, California. The clinical-stage biopharmaceutical company develops medicines consisting of a pipeline of small molecule product candidates that target cancer. The company's lead product candidate is an orally bioavailable inhibitor of farnesyl transferase that is in phase 2 clinical trials for the treatment of solid tumors, peripheral T-cell lymphomas, and other hematologic malignancies. They are also developing a small molecule inhibitor of extracellular signal-related kinase used for the treatment of patients with tumors that have dysregulated activity due to mutations or other mechanisms in the mitogen-activated protein kinase pathway and KO-539, a small molecule inhibitor of the menin-mixed lineage leukemia protein-protein interaction. Kura Oncology, Inc. was founded in 2014. Over a five-year period, the company's stock price fluctuated between the low of $7.70/share and the high of $41.62/share.

MEI Pharma, Inc. (https://investor.meipharma.com/), whose stock ticker is MEIP, trades on NasdaqCM (Capital Market) and is based in San Diego, California. The late-stage pharmaceutical company focuses on the development of various therapies for the treatment of cancer. The company's clinical drug candidate includes an oral available histone deacetylase inhibitor for the treatment of patients with acute myeloid leukemia (AML) and myelodysplastic syndrome. Their clinical development portfolio also includes an oral inhibitor of phosphatidylinositide 3-kinase delta for the treatment of patients with relapsed/refractory follicular lymphoma and B-cell malignancies and an oral cyclin-dependent kinase inhibitor for B-cell malignancies and AML. In addition, the company engages in the development of a mitochondrial inhibitor targeting the oxidative phosphorylation complex for the treatment of HER2-negative breast cancer. Over a five-year period, the company's stock price fluctuated between the low of $0.34/share and the high of $4.95/share.

Mersana Therapeutics, Inc. (http://ir.mersana.com/), whose stock ticker is MRSN, trades on NasdaqGS (Global Select) and is based in Cambridge, Massachusetts. The clinical-stage biopharmaceutical company focuses on the development of antibody drug conjugate (ADC) for cancer patients with unmet needs. The company develops a platform that is used to generate a pipeline of proprietary ADC product candidates to address patient populations that are not amenable to treat with traditional ADC-based therapies. Their lead product candidate is a Dolaflexin ADC targeting NaPi2b that is in phase 1 clinical trial for the treatment of patients with ovarian cancer, nonsmall cell lung cancer, and other orphan indications. Over a five-year period, the company's stock price fluctuated between the low of $1.51/share and the high of $26.61/share.

NanoString Technologies, Inc. (http://investors.nanostring.com/), whose stock ticker is NSTG, trades on NasdaqGS (Global Select) and is headquartered in Seattle, Washington. The company provides life science tools for translational research and molecular diagnostic products worldwide. The company offers an automated, multiapplication, digital detection, and counting system, including an automated liquid handling component that processes and prepares samples for data collection. And it provides nCounter Digital Analyzer, which collects data from samples by taking images of the immobilized fluorescent reporters in the sample cartridge and processing the data into output files. The company also offers an instrument that provides liquid handling steps and the digital analysis through use of a microfluidic cartridge and a data analysis program that enables researchers to check, normalize, and analyze their data. In addition, they provide custom CodeSets as well as Pan Cancer and 360 gene expression, CAR-T characterization, protein immune profiling, neuropathology and neuro-inflammation gene expression, Mouse-AD, autoimmune disease gene expression, miRNA expression, and other gene expression panels. Over a five-year period, the company's stock price fluctuated between the low of $6.47/share and the high of $82.96/share.

Radius Health Inc. (https://ir.radiuspharm.com/), whose stock ticker is RDUS, trades on NasdaqGM (Global Market) and is headquartered in Waltham, Massachusetts. The biopharmaceutical company develops and commercializes endocrine therapeutics in the areas of osteoporosis and oncology. The company markets Elacestrant (RAD1901), a selective estrogen receptor degrader that is in phase 3 clinical study for the treatment of hormone receptor-positive breast cancer and RAD140, a nonsteroidal selective androgen receptor modulator that is in phase 1A clinical study to treat metastatic breast cancer. From 2016 to 2021, the stock price fluctuated between the high of $47/share (July 2017) down to $7/share (December 2021).

Sorrento Therapeutics (http://investors.sorrentotherapeutics.com/), whose stock ticker is SRNE, trades on NasdaqGS (Global

Select) and is based in San Diego, California. The clinical-stage biotechnology company primarily engages in the discovery and development of therapies focused on oncology and the treatment of chronic cancer pain worldwide. The company offers a non-opioid based TRPV1 agonist neurotoxin for the treatment of intractable pain treatment and a lidocaine delivery system for the treatment of postherpetic neuralgia. They also develop CD38 Directed chimeric antigen receptor T-cell therapy (CAR-T) for the treatment of multiple myeloma as well as for amyloidosis and graft-versus-host diseases and carcinoembryonic antigen CAR-T cell therapy for the treatment of liver metastases of pancreatic cancer. Over a five-year period, the company's stock price fluctuated between the low of $1.43/share and the high of $14.42/share.

Verastem (https://www.verastem.com/investors/), whose stock ticker is VSTM, trades on NasdaqGS (Global Select) and is headquartered in Needham, Massachusetts. The biopharmaceutical company focuses on developing and commercializing medicines to improve the survival and quality of life of cancer patients. They market products for the treatment of adult patients with relapsed or refractory chronic lymphocytic leukemia/small lymphocytic lymphoma after at least two prior therapies and relapsed or refractory follicular lymphoma (FL) after at least two prior systemic therapies. In addition, they are developing immunotherapeutic agents for the treatment of various cancer types, including pancreatic cancer, ovarian cancer, nonsmall cell lung cancer (NSCLC), mesothelioma, and other solid tumors. Over a five-year period, the company's stock price fluctuated between the low of $0.31/share and the high of $9.96/share.

ViewRay, Inc. (http://investors.viewray.com/), whose stock ticker is VRAY, trades on NasdaqGS (Global Select) and is headquartered in Oakwood, Ohio. The company designs, manufactures, and markets radiation therapy systems. They offer a magnetic resonance image-guided radiation therapy system to image and treat cancer patients and integrate MRI technology, radiation delivery, and proprietary software to see the soft tissues, shape the dose to accommodate for changes in anatomy, and strike the target using real-time targeting throughout the treatment. The company serves university research and teaching hospitals, community hospitals, private practices, government institutions, and freestanding cancer centers. The company markets their products through a direct sales force in North America. It has operations in the United States, France, Germany, Taiwan, the United Kingdom, and other countries. Over a five-year period, the company's stock price fluctuated between the low of $1.35/share and the high of $11.04/share.

Mid Cap Companies

(Greater than $2 Billion, up to $10 Billion)

Arcus Biosciences, Inc. (https://investors.arcusbio.com/investors/investor-relations/default.aspx), whose stock ticker is RCUS, trades on the NYSE. The company, based in Hayward, California, is a clinical-stage biopharmaceutical company that engages in developing and commercializing cancer immunotherapies in the United States. The company develops various programs targeting immuno-oncology pathways, including a dual adenosine receptor antagonist and an antibody. Over a five-year period, the company's stock price fluctuated between the low of $6.84/share and the high of $47.55/share.

    Blueprint Medicines (http://ir.blueprintmedicines.com/), whose stock ticker is BPMC, trades on NasdaqGS (Global Select) and is based in Cambridge, Massachusetts. The company develops drugs of small molecule kinase inhibitors that target genomic drivers in various cancers and a rare genetic disease such as hepatocellular carcinoma. It is also developing an orally available and potent inhibitor that targets RET, a receptor tyrosine kinase that is abnormally activated by mutations or translocations and RET resistant mutants that would arise from treatment with first generation therapies. In addition, the company is developing an inhibitor targeting the kinase ALK2 for the treatment of fibrodysplasia ossificans progressiva, a rare genetic disease caused by mutations in the ALK2 gene, ACVR1. The company was founded in 2008. Over a five-year period, the company's stock price fluctuated between the low of $45.57/share and the high of $123.64/share.

Crispr Therapeutics (https://crisprtx.gcs-web.com/), whose stock ticker is CRSP, trades on NasdaqGM (Global Market) and is based in Zug, Switzerland. It is a gene-editing company that focuses on developing transformative gene-based medicines for serious diseases. The company develops their products using a revolutionary gene editing technology that allows for precise directed changes to genomic DNA. It has a portfolio of therapeutic programs in a range of disease areas, including hemoglobinopathies, oncology, regenerative medicine, and rare diseases. The company is also developing a donor-derived, gene-edited allogeneic CAR-T therapy targeting cluster of differentiation 19 positive malignancies. In addition, it is developing allogeneic CAR-T programs targeting B-cell maturation antigen for the treatment of multiple myeloma and for the treatment of solid tumors and hematologic malignancies. Over a five-year period, the company's stock price fluctuated between the low of $18.95/share and the high of $199.88/share.

Exact Sciences Corporation (http://investor.exactsciences.com/investor-relations/default.aspx), whose stock ticker is EXAS, trades on NasdaqCM (Capital Market) and is based in Madison, Wisconsin. The molecular diagnostics company focuses on developing products for the early detection and prevention of various cancers in the United States. The company offers a non-invasive, stool-based DNA screening test for the early detection of colorectal cancer and precancer. Over a five-year period, the company's stock price fluctuated between the low of $30.35/share and the high of $155.01/share.

Exelixis, Inc. (https://ir.exelixis.com/investors-overview), whose stock ticker is EXEL, trades on NasdaqGS (Global Select) and is based in Alameda, California. The oncology-focused biotechnology company focuses on the discovery, development, and commercialization of new medicines to treat cancers in the United States. The company's products include tablets for the treatment of patients with advanced renal cell carcinoma who received prior anti-angiogenic therapy and capsules for the treatment of patients with progressive and metastatic medullary thyroid cancer. The company is developing drugs to treat advanced solid tumors, including genitourinary cancers, as a monotherapy and in combination with immune checkpoint inhibitors. The company also offers an inhibitor to treat advanced melanoma. Over a five-year period, the company's stock price fluctuated between the low of $14.38/share and the high of $31.62/share.

Guardant Health, Inc. (https://investors.guardanthealth.com/), whose stock ticker is GH, trades on NasdaqGS (Global Select) and is headquartered in Redwood City, California. The precision oncology company provides blood tests, data sets, and analytics in the United States and other countries. The company offers liquid biopsy tests for advanced stage cancer such as Guardant360, a molecular diagnostic test that measures various cancer-related genes, and GuardantOMNI, a broader gene panel, including genes associated with homologous recombination repair deficiency and biomarkers for immuno-oncology applications. It also provides LUNAR-1 for minimal residual disease and recurrence detection in cancer survivors. In addition, the company is developing LUNAR-2 for early detection of cancer in higher risk individuals. They have a collaboration agreement with Radius Health, Inc. to develop liquid biopsy companion diagnostic for elacestrant. Over a five-year period, the company's stock price fluctuated between the low of $29.20/share and the high of $179.10/share.

Halozyme Therapeutics, Inc. (https://www.halozyme.com/investors/default.aspx), whose stock ticker is HALO, trades on NasdaqGS (Global Select) and is based in San Diego. The biotechnology company engages in researching, developing, and commercializing oncology therapies in the United States, Switzerland, and other countries. The company's products are based on a patented recombinant human hyaluronidase enzyme (rHuPH20) that enables the subcutaneous delivery of injectable biologics, such as monoclonal antibodies and other therapeutic molecules, as well as small molecules and fluids. The company also develops a therapy that is in clinical trial for pancreatic cancer, in clinical trial for nonsmall cell lung cancer, in clinical trial for patients with previously treated metastatic pancreatic ductal adenocarcinoma, in clinical trial for patients with gastric cancer, and in clinical trial for cholangiocarcinoma and gall bladder cancer. Over a five-year period, the company's stock price fluctuated between the low of $13.89/share and the high of $51.78/share.

Integer Holdings Corporation (https://investor.integer.net/investor-relations/default.aspx), whose stock ticker is ITGR, trades on NYSE and is based in Plano, Texas. The company operates as a medical device outsource manufacturer in the United States, Puerto Rico, Costa Rica, and other countries. They operate in two segments: medical and nonmedical. The company offers products for interventional cardiology, structural heart, heart failure, peripheral vascular, neurovascular, interventional oncology, electrophysiology, vascular access, infusion therapy, hemodialysis, urology, and gastroenterology procedures. The company was formerly known as Greatbatch, Inc. and changed its name to Integer Holdings Corporation in July 2016. Integer Holdings Corporation was founded in 1970. Over a five-year period, the company's stock price fluctuated between the low of $44.15/share and the high of $98.30/share.

Iovance Biotherapeutics, Inc. (http://ir.iovance.com/), whose stock ticker is IOVA, trades on NasdaqGM (Global Market) and is based in San Carlos, California. The clinical-stage biotechnology company focuses on developing and commercializing cancer immunotherapy products to harness the power of a patient's immune system to eradicate cancer cells. They seek the development and commercialization of novel cancer immunotherapies related to ovarian, breast, bladder, and colorectal cancers. The company's lead product candidate is an adoptive cell therapy that is in clinical trial using tumor-infiltrating lymphocytes (TIL) that are T cells derived from patients' tumors for the treatment of metastatic melanoma. The company is also developing an autologous adoptive cell therapy to treat cervical and head and neck cancers. Over a five-year period, the company's stock price fluctuated between the low of $7.02/share and the high of $51.06/share.

Jazz Pharmaceuticals (https://investor.jazzpharma.com/investors), whose stock ticker is JAZZ, trades on NasdaqGS (Global Select) and is headquartered in Dublin, Ireland. The biopharmaceutical company identifies, develops, and commercializes pharmaceutical products for various unmet medical needs in the United States, Europe, and other regions. The company has a portfolio of products and product candidates with a focus in the areas of neuroscience, including oncology and hematologic and solid tumors. Their lead marketed products include Erwinaze to treat acute lymphoblastic leukemia, Vyxeos liposome for the treatment of adults with newly diagnosed therapy-related acute myeloid leukemia, and Zepzelca for the treatment of adult patients with metastatic small cell lung cancer. Jazz Pharmaceuticals PLC has licensing and collaboration agreements with ImmunoGen, Inc., Codiak BioSciences, Inc., Pfenex, Inc., XL-protein GmBH, and Redx Pharma PLC. Over a five-year period, the company's stock price fluctuated between the low of $96.13/share and the high of $186.17/share.

Ligand Pharmaceuticals (https://investor.ligand.com/), whose stock ticker is LGND, trades on NasdaqGM (Global Market) and is headquartered in San Diego, California. The biopharmaceutical company focuses on developing and acquiring technologies that help pharmaceutical companies discover and develop medicines worldwide. Their commercial programs include an oral medicine that increases the number of platelets in the blood, medicines used to treat multiple myeloma, and drugs for nonsmall cell lung cancer. The company conducts clinical trials for the treatment of seizure, coma, cancer, diabetes, cardiovascular diseases, muscle wasting, liver and kidney diseases, and others. Over a five-year period, the company's stock price fluctuated between the low of $66.79/share and the high of $274.49/share.

Mirati Therapeutics Inc. (https://ir.mirati.com/overview/default.aspx), whose stock ticker is MRTX, trades on NasdaqGS (Global Select) and based in San Diego, California. The clinical-stage oncology company develops product candidates to address the genetic and immunological promoters of cancer in the United States. The company participates in developing a spectrum-selective kinase inhibitor that is in clinical trials for the treatment of nonsmall cell lung cancer (NCSLC) and in clinical trials to treat NCSLC patients with Casitas B-lineage lymphoma genetic alterations. The company has also developed an inhibitor program for NSCLC adenocarcinoma patients, colorectal cancer patients, and other cancer patients. Over a five-year period, the company's stock price fluctuated between the low of $13.00/share and the high of $238.29/share.

Nektar Therapeutics (https://ir.nektar.com/), whose stock ticker is NKTR, trades on NasdaqGS (Global Select) and is headquartered in San Francisco, California. The company develops drug candidates for cancer, auto-immune disease, and chronic pain in the United States. The company develops an orally available mu-opioid analgesic molecule for moderate to severe chronic pain, a topoisomerase 1 inhibitor that is in clinical trial for advanced metastatic breast cancer in patients with brain metastases, and a CD122-preferential interleukin-2 (IL-2) pathway agonist to treat immuno-oncology. It also develops a cytokine Treg stimulant that is in clinical trial to treat autoimmune diseases and a toll-like receptor agonist that is in phase 1 for solid tumors and immuno-oncology. In addition, it is developing products for nonsmall cell lung cancer and other tumor types as well as longer-acting blood-clotting proteins for hemophilia. Over a five-year period, the company's stock price fluctuated between the low of $3.32/share and the high of $108.34/share.

NeoGenomics, Inc. (https://ir.neogenomics.com/), whose stock ticker is NEO, trades on NasdaqGS (Global Select) and is headquartered in Fort Myers, Florida. Together with their subsidiaries, the company operates a network of cancer-focused genetic testing laboratories in the United States and other laboratories in Switzerland and Singapore. The company's laboratories provide genetic and molecular testing services to hospitals, pathologists, oncologists, urologists, other clinicians and researchers, pharmaceutical firms, academic centers, and other clinical laboratories. They offer cytogenetics testing services to study normal and abnormal chromosomes and their relationship to diseases and fluorescence in situ hybridization testing services that focus on detecting and locating the presence or absence of specific DNA sequences and genes on chromosomes. In addition, the company offers flow cytometry testing services to measure the characteristics of cell populations, immunohistochemistry, and digital imaging testing services to localize proteins in cells of a tissue section as well as to allow clients to see and utilize scanned slides and perform quantitative analysis for various stains. NeoGenomics offers molecular testing services that focus on the analysis of DNA and RNA as well as the structure and function of genes at the molecular level. Over a five-year period, the company's stock price fluctuated between the low of $6.45/share and the high of $59.88/share.

NovoCure Limited (https://www.novocure.com/investor-relations/), whose stock ticker is NVCR, trades on NasdaqGS (Global Select) and is based in Saint Helier, Jersey, UK. The company has US operations in Portsmouth, New Hampshire, and New York, New York, with additional offices in Germany, Switzerland, Japan, and a research center in Haifa, Israel. The company offers cancer therapy that uses electronic fields tuned to specific frequencies to disrupt cell division, inhibiting tumor growth and potentially causing cancer cells to die. The company markets a Tumor Treating Fields delivery system for use as a monotherapy treatment for adult patients with glioblastoma. They are also developing products for brain metastases, nonsmall cell lung cancer, pancreatic cancer, gastric cancer, ovarian cancer, liver cancer, and mesothelioma. Over a five-year period, the company's stock price fluctuated between the low of $17.30/share and the high of $221.25/share.

PTC Therapeutics, Inc. (http://ir.ptcbio.com/investor-relations), whose stock ticker is PTCT, trades on NasdaqGS (Global Select) and is headquartered in South Plainfield, New Jersey. The biopharmaceutical company focuses on the discovery, development, and commercialization of medicines for the treatment of rare disorders. Their portfolio pipeline includes commercial products and product candidates in various stages of development, including clinical, preclinical, and research and discovery stages. The company focuses on the development of treatments for multiple therapeutic areas, including rare diseases and oncology. The company is in clinical development stage to treat cancer patients. Over a five-year period, the company's stock price fluctuated between the low of $15.78/share and the high of $68.49/share.

Teva Pharmaceutical Industries Limited (https://ir.tevapharm.com/investors/default.aspx), whose stock ticker is TEVA, trades on NYSE and is headquartered in Petach Tikva, Israel. The company develops, manufactures, markets, and distributes generic medicines, specialty medicines, and biopharmaceutical products in North America, Europe, and other regions. The company offers sterile products, hormones, high-potency drugs, and cytotoxic substances in various dosage forms, including tablets, capsules, injectables, inhalants, liquids, ointments, and creams. They also develop, manufacture, and sell active pharmaceutical ingredients. In addition, the company provides specialty medicines for use in central nervous system and respiratory indications and products in the oncology market. Teva Pharmaceutical Industries Limited was founded in 1901. Over a five-year period, the company's stock price fluctuated between the low of $6.41/share and the high of $24.36/share.

Large Cap Companies
(Greater than $10 Billion, up to $200 Billion)

Abbott Laboratories (https://www.abbott.com/investors.html), whose stock ticker is ABT, trades on the NYSE. The company is based in Abbott Park, Illinois, and discovers, develops, manufactures, and sells healthcare products worldwide. The firm offers pharmaceuticals for the treatment of chronic myeloid leukemia, pancreatic exocrine insufficiency, irritable bowel syndrome or biliary spasm, intrahepatic cholestasis or depressive symptom, and gynecological disorders. Abbott Laboratories is also a leader in glucose monitoring, blood and plasma screening, adult and pediatric nutrition, heart pump technologies, remote heart failure monitoring, post-op care testing, and chronic pain technologies. Over a five-year period, the company's stock price fluctuated between the low of $54.80/share and the high of $140.74/share.

Amgen Inc. (http://investors.amgen.com/), whose stock ticker is AMGN, trades on NasdaqGS (Global Select) and is based in Thousand Oaks, California. Amgen discovers, develops, manufactures, and delivers human therapeutics worldwide. Their product offerings include treatment related to oncology/hematology, cardiovascular, inflammation, bone health, and neuroscience. The company's products treat plaque psoriasis, rheumatoid arthritis, psoriatic arthritis, and cancer postmenopausal symptoms, such as osteoporosis and anemia. Amgen also focuses on treating chronic kidney disease and lower than normal red blood cell counts. Over a five-year period, the company's stock price fluctuated between the low of $166.70/share and the high of $258.46/share.

AstraZeneca PLC, (https://www.astrazeneca.com/investor-relations.html), whose stock ticker is AZN, has their primary listing on the London Stock Exchange and is a constituent of the FTSE 100 Index. The company has their secondary listings on Nasdaq. The firm is based in Cambridge, UK, and discovers, develops, and commercializes prescription medicines in the areas of oncology, cardiovascular, renal and metabolism, respiratory, autoimmunity, infection, neuroscience, and gastroenterology worldwide. AstraZeneca serves primary care and specialty care physicians through distributors and local representative offices. Over a five-year period, the company's stock price fluctuated between the low of $32.85/share and the high of $71.14/share.

BioNTech SE (https://investors.biontech.de/), whose stock ticker is BNTX, trades on NasdaqGS (Global Select) and is headquartered in Mainz, Germany. It is a biotechnology company that develops and commercializes immunotherapies for cancer and other infectious diseases. The company engages in developing clinical trials for advanced melanoma, prostate cancer, head and neck cancer, breast cancer, ovarian cancer, and nonsmall cell lung cancer. It also develops neoantigen specific immunotherapies for first-line melanoma and multiple solid tumors, pancreatic and other cancers. BioNTech SE is also in clinical trials related to infectious disease immunotherapies and rare disease protein replacement therapies. The company has collaborations with Genentech, Inc.; Sanofi SA; Genmab A/S; Genevant Sciences GmbH; Eli Lilly and Company; Bayer AG; Pfizer Inc.; Shanghai Fosun Pharmaceutical (Group) Co., Ltd.; Regeneron Pharmaceuticals, Inc.; and InstaDeep Ltd. Over a five-year period, the company's stock price fluctuated between the low of $13.82/share and the high of $389.01/share.

Bristol-Myers Squibb (https://www.bms.com/investors/stock-information.html), whose stock ticker is BMY, trades on NYSE and is based in New York, New York. The company discovers, develops, licenses, manufactures, markets, distributes, and sells biopharmaceutical products worldwide. They offer drugs in oncology, immunoscience, cardiovascular, and fibrotic diseases. The company's products include a biological product for anticancer indications, an oral inhibitor targeted at stroke prevention in adult patients with nonvalvular atrial fibrillation, and the prevention and treatment of venous thromboembolic disorders and severely active polyarticular juvenile idiopathic arthritis. They also provide a tyrosine kinase inhibitor for the treatment of Philadelphia chromosome-positive chronic myeloid leukemia, a monoclonal antibody for the treatment of patients with unresectable or metastatic melanoma, and a humanized monoclonal antibody for the treatment of multiple myeloma. Over a five-year period, the company's stock price fluctuated between the low of $43.33/share and the high of $78.96/share.

Gilead Sciences, Inc. (http://investors.gilead.com/), whose stock ticker is GILD, trades on NasdaqGS (Global Select) and is based in Foster City, California. It is a research-based biopharmaceutical company that discovers, develops, and commercializes medicines in the areas of unmet medical needs in the United States, Europe, and other regions. Gilead Sciences also entered the oncology market in 2017 by acquiring Kite Pharma and their cellular-based cancer therapies. The company provides a chimeric antigen receptor T cell therapy for adult patients with relapsed or refractory large B-cell lymphoma. Over a five-year period, the company's stock price fluctuated between the low of $57.07/share and the high of $85.46/share.

GlaxoSmithKline (GSK PLC) (https://www.gsk.com/en-gb/investors/), whose stock ticker is GSK, trades on the London Stock Exchange and is based in Brentford, UK. The company engages in the creation, discovery, development, manufacture, and marketing of pharmaceutical products, vaccines, over-the-counter medicines, and health-related consumer products in the United Kingdom, the United States, and other countries. GSK's research and development has focused on using cutting-edge treatments for cancer patients. Their focus includes immuno-oncology (using the human immune system to treat cancer), cell therapy (engineering human T-cells to target cancer), cancer epigenetics (modulating the epigenome, the information that directs how DNA is read and used, to induce anticancer effects), and synthetic lethality (addressing two targets at the same time which together, but not alone, have substantial effects against cancer). The company was formerly known as

GlaxoSmithKline PLC and changed its official name to GSK PLC in May 2022. Over a five-year period, the company's stock price fluctuated between the low of $29.43/share and the high of $47.89/share.

Illumina, Inc. (https://investor.illumina.com/investors/default.aspx), whose stock ticker is ILMN, trades on NasdaqGS (Global Select) and is headquartered in San Diego, California. The company provides sequencing and array-based solutions for genetic and genomic analysis. Their products and services serve customers in a range of markets, enabling the adoption of genomic solutions in research and clinical settings for applications in the life sciences, oncology, reproductive health, agriculture, and other emerging segments. The company provides instruments and consumables used in genetic analysis, genotyping and sequencing services, instrument service contracts, and development and licensing agreements. Their customers include genomic research centers, academic institutions, government laboratories, and hospitals as well as pharmaceutical, biotechnology, commercial molecular diagnostic laboratories, and consumer genomics companies. Illumina markets and distributes their products directly to customers in North America, Europe, Latin America, and the Asia-Pacific region and sells through life-science distributors in certain markets within Europe, the Asia-Pacific region, Latin America, the Middle East, and Africa. Over a five-year period, the company's stock price fluctuated between the low of $187.29/share and the high of $517.32/share.

Incyte Corporation (https://investor.incyte.com/), whose stock tickers is INCY, trades on NasdaqGS (Global Select) and is based in Wilmington, Delaware. The biopharmaceutical company focuses on the discovery, development, and commercialization of various therapeutics in the United States. The company offers a drug to treat chronic myeloid leukemia and Philadelphia-chromosome positive acute lymphoblastic leukemia. Their clinical-stage products combat steroid-refractory acute graft-versus-host-diseases and treat essential thrombocythemia and refractory myelofibrosis. In addition, Incyte engages in the development of clinical trials to treat naïve acute and chronic graft-versus-host-diseases as well as clinical trials for nonsmall cell lung cancer. The company also completes clinical trials for treating bladder cancer and bile duct cancer as well as a pivotal program for solid tumors with driver activations. Furthermore, the company engages in developing clinical trials for MSI-high endometrial cancer, Merkel cell carcinoma, and anal cancer and has developed clinical trials for follicular lymphoma, marginal zone lymphoma, and mantle cell lymphoma. Over a five-year period, the company's stock price fluctuated between the low of $58.67/share and the high of $116.27/share.

LabCorp Corporation of America Holdings (https://ir.labcorp.com/), whose stock ticker is LH, trades on NYSE and is headquartered in Burlington, North Carolina. They operate as an independent clinical laboratory company worldwide that offers various clinical laboratory tests, such as blood chemistry analyses, urinalyses, blood cell counts, thyroid tests, Pap tests, hemoglobin A1C and vitamin D products, prostate-specific antigens, tests for sexually transmitted diseases, hepatitis C tests, microbiology cultures and procedures, and alcohol- and other substance-abuse tests. The company also provides testing services in the areas of women's health, allergy, diagnostic genetics, cardiovascular disease, infectious disease, endocrinology, oncology, coagulation, pharmacogenetics, toxicology, medical drug monitoring, esoteric testing, cancer diagnostics, and other complex procedures. Furthermore, it offers end-to-end drug development, medical devices, and diagnostic development solutions from research to clinical development and commercial market access. Over a five-year period, the company's stock price fluctuated between the low of $107.24/share and the high of $314.21/share.

Moderna, Inc. (https://investors.modernatx.com/), whose stock ticker is MRNA, trades on NasdaqGS (Global Select) and is headquartered in Cambridge, Massachusetts. The clinical-stage biotechnology company develops therapeutics and vaccines based on messenger RNA for the treatment of infectious diseases, immuno-oncology, rare diseases, and cardiovascular diseases. As of February 15, 2019, the company had programs in clinical trials and a total of twenty development candidates in six modalities comprising prophylactic vaccines, cancer vaccines, intratumoral immuno-oncology, localized regenerative therapeutics, systemic secreted therapeutics, and systemic intracellular therapeutics. Moderna has strategic alliances with AstraZeneca, Merck & Co., Vertex Pharmaceuticals, Biomedical Advanced Research and Development Authority, Defense Advanced Research Projects Agency, the Bill & Melinda Gates Foundation, and a research collaboration with Harvard University. Moderna, Inc. also has collaborations with Lonza Ltd. for the manufacture of mRNA-1273, a COVID-19 vaccine, and Catalent for fill-finish manufacturing of their COVID-19 vaccine candidate. The company was formerly known as Moderna Therapeutics, Inc. and changed its name to Moderna, Inc. in August 2018. Over a five-year period, the company's stock price fluctuated between the low of $12.73/share and the high of $449.38/share.

Novartis AG (https://www.novartis.com/investors), whose stock ticker is NVS, trades on NYSE and is headquartered in Basel, Switzerland. The company completes research, develops, manufactures, and markets healthcare products worldwide. The company's Innovative Medicines segment offers prescription medicines for patients and healthcare providers. They also offer ophthalmology, neuroscience, immunology, hepatology and dermatology, respiratory, cardio-metabolic, and established medicine products. The company's Sandoz segment provides active ingredients and finished dosage forms of pharmaceuticals in cardiovascular, central nervous system, dermatology, gastrointestinal and hormonal therapy, metabolism, oncology, ophthalmic, pain, and respiratory areas, and finished dosage form anti-infective. Over a five-year period, the company's stock price fluctuated between the low of $67.26/share and the high of $97.63/share.

Quest Diagnostics Incorporated (https://ir.questdiagnostics.

com/overview/default.aspx), whose stock ticker is DGX, trades on NYSE and is headquartered in Secaucus, New Jersey. The company provides diagnostic testing, information, and services in the United States and other countries. The company develops and delivers diagnostic testing information and services, such as routine testing, nonroutine and advanced clinical testing, anatomic pathology testing, and other diagnostic information services. It offers diagnostic information services primarily under the Quest Diagnostics brand, as well as under the AmeriPath, Dermpath Diagnostics, Athena Diagnostics, ExamOne, and Quanum brands to patients, clinicians, hospitals, integrated delivery networks, health plans, employers, and accountable care organizations through a network of laboratories. The company also offers patient service centers, phlebotomists in physician offices, call centers and mobile paramedics, nurses, and other health and wellness professional services. Over a five-year period, the company's stock price fluctuated between the low of $73.34/share and the high of $173.01/share.

Regeneron Pharmaceuticals, Inc. (https://investor.regeneron.com/investor-relations), whose stock ticker is REGN, trades on NasdaqGM (Global) and is headquartered in Tarrytown, New York. The biopharmaceutical company discovers, invents, develops, manufactures, and commercializes medicines for treating various medical conditions worldwide. The company offers Libtayo injection to treat metastatic or locally advanced cutaneous squamous cell carcinoma and metastatic colorectal cancer. Furthermore, they are developing various product candidates for treating patients with eye diseases, allergic and inflammatory diseases, cancer, cardiovascular and metabolic diseases, neuromuscular diseases, and infectious diseases. Over a five-year period, the company's stock price fluctuated between the low of $274.46/share and the high of $738.84/share.

Sanofi (https://www.sanofi.com/en/investors/sanofi-share-and-adrs/share-overview), whose stock ticker is SNY, trades on NasdaqGS (Global Select) and is headquartered in Paris, France. The company provides therapeutic solutions worldwide and offers products for metastatic cutaneous squamous cell carcinoma and hematologic malignancies including metastatic colorectal cancer. The company also provides generic products and products for allergy, cough, cold, pain, nutrition, digestion, pediatrics, influenza, meningitis, and travel and produces endemic vaccines and adult and adolescent boosters. Sanofi also engages in collaborative work with the private company TrialSpark Inc. to execute clinical research studies related to chronic obstructive pulmonary disease. Over a five-year period, the company's stock price fluctuated between the low of $38.02/share and the high of $56.75/share.

Seagen, Inc. (https://investor.seagen.com/overview/default.aspx), whose stock ticker is SGEN, trades on NasdaqGS (Global Select) and is headquartered in Bothell, Washington. The biotechnology company develops and commercializes therapies for the treatment of cancer in the United States and other countries. The company markets an antibody-drug conjugate (ADC) for the treatment of patients with Hodgkin lymphoma or CD30-positive T-cell lymphomas. Seagen also conducts various clinical trials to evaluate and treat patients with relapsed or refractory, or transplant-ineligible, advanced classical Hodgkin lymphoma, relapsed or refractory B-cell and T-cell non-Hodgkin lymphomas, second-line Hodgkin lymphoma, and relapsed/refractory classical Hodgkin lymphoma. In addition, the company develops an ADC composed of an anti-Nectin-4 monoclonal antibody to treat bladder cancer, ovarian cancer, and lung cancer. They developed an oral tyrosine kinase inhibitor for HER2-positive metastatic breast cancer and an ADC composed of a human antibody that binds to tissue factor to treat various solid tumors, including cervical, ovarian, prostate, and bladder. Furthermore, they develop early-stage clinical trials for metastatic triple-negative breast cancer and products for patients with relapsed or refractory multiple myeloma and advanced solid tumors. The company was formerly known as Seattle Genetics, Inc. and changed its name to Seagen Inc. in October 2020. The company was incorporated in 1997. Over a five-year period, the company's stock price fluctuated between the low of $50.07/share and the high of $200.78/share.

Teledoc Health, Inc. (https://ir.teladochealth.com/investors/default.aspx), whose stock ticker is TDOC, trades on NYSE and is headquartered in Purchase, New York. The company provides virtual healthcare services on a business-to-business basis in the United States and other countries. They cover various clinical conditions, including noncritical, episodic care, chronic, and complicated cases like cancer and congestive heart failure. They also offer telehealth solutions, expert medical services, behavioral health solutions, guidance and support, and platform and program services. The company's platform enables patients and providers to have an integrated smart user experience through mobile, web, and phone-based accessed points. They serve health employers, health plans, hospitals, health systems, and insurance and financial services companies. The company was formerly known as Teladoc, Inc. and changed their name to Teladoc Health, Inc. in August 2018. Over a five-year period, the company's stock price fluctuated between the low of $23.16/share and the high of $293.66/share.

Vertex Pharmaceuticals Incorporated (https://investors.vrtx.com/), whose stock ticker is VRTX, trades on NasdaqGS (Global Select) and is headquartered in Boston, Massachusetts. The company engages primarily in developing and commercializing therapies for treating cystic fibrosis. However, the company has collaborated with other notable biotech firms, such as Merck and others, in various clinical research initiatives and treatments related to oncology. Their pipeline includes products for treatment for serious kidney diseases. The company sells its products primarily to specialty pharmacy and specialty distributors in the United States as well as to specialty distributors and retail chains, and hospitals and clinics internationally. Vertex Pharmaceuticals Incorporated has collaborations with other notable firms that treat cancer, including with CRISPR Therapeutics AG and Moderna, Inc. They also have a strategic research collaboration and licensing agreement with

Obsidian Therapeutics, Inc. for the discovery of novel therapies that regulate gene editing for the treatment of serious diseases. Over a five-year period, the company's stock price fluctuated between the low of $140.79/share and the high of $300.00/share.

Mega Cap Companies

(Greater than $200 Billion; Generally
Lowest Stock Price Volatility)

Abbvie Inc. (https://investors.abbvie.com/), whose stock ticker is ABBV, trades on the NYSE. The company is based in Chicago, Illinois, and discovers, develops, manufactures, and sells pharmaceutical products in the United States, Japan, Germany, Canada, Italy, Spain, the Netherlands, the UK, Brazil, and other countries. The company offers products that treat autoimmune and intestinal diseases, chronic lymphocytic leukemia (CLL), small lymphocytic lymphoma (SLL), mantle cell lymphoma, marginal zone lymphoma, and chronic graft-versus-host disease. The company develops drugs that treat prostate cancer, endometriosis, and central precocious puberty as well as anemia. To bolster their growth outlook, AbbVie in 2015 bought biotech firm Pharmacyclics, which developed the blood-cancer treatment Imbruvica in partnership with Johnson & Johnson. Over a five-year period, the company's stock price fluctuated between the low of $64.43/share and the high of $174.96/share.

Johnson & Johnson (http://www.investor.jnj.com/), whose stock ticker is JNJ, trades on NYSE and is based in New Brunswick, New Jersey. Together with their subsidiaries, the company researches, develops, manufactures, and sells various products in the healthcare field worldwide. They operate in three segments: consumer, pharmaceutical, and medical devices. The pharmaceutical segment offers products in various therapeutic areas, including immunology, infectious diseases, neuroscience, oncology, pulmonary hypertension, and cardiovascular and metabolic diseases. The company markets their products to public and retail outlets and distributors, as well as distributes directly to wholesalers, hospitals, and healthcare professionals for prescription use. Over a five-year period, the company's stock price fluctuated between the low of $119.89/share and the high of $189.29/share.

Eli Lilly and Company (https://investor.lilly.com/investor-relations), whose stock ticker is LLY, trades on NYSE and is based in Indianapolis, Indiana. The company discovers, develops, manufactures, and markets pharmaceutical products worldwide. The company offers oncology products to treat nonsmall cell lung, colorectal, head and neck, pancreatic, metastatic breast, ovarian, bladder, and metastatic gastric cancers, as well as malignant pleural mesothelioma. Over a five-year period, the company's stock price fluctuated between the low of $74.76/share and the high of $340.77/share.

Merck & Co., Inc. (https://investors.merck.com/home/default.aspx), whose stock ticker is MRK, trades on NYSE and is headquartered in Kenilworth, New Jersey. The company provides healthcare solutions worldwide and offers products to prevent chemotherapy-induced and postoperative nausea and vomiting and to treat nonsmall cell lung, ovarian, breast, thyroid, cervical, and brain cancers. Merck seeks to prevent diseases caused by human papillomavirus, as well as offers vaccines for measles, mumps, rubella, varicella, shingles, rotavirus gastroenteritis, and pneumococcal diseases. In addition, the company provides antibiotic and anti-inflammatory drugs to treat infectious and respiratory diseases, fertility disorders, and pneumonia. Over a five-year period, the company's stock price fluctuated between the low of $50.92/share and the high of $95.67/share.

Pfizer Inc. (https://investors.pfizer.com/investors-overview/default.aspx), whose stock ticker is PFE, trades on NYSE and is headquartered in New York, New York. The company develops, manufactures, and sells healthcare products worldwide. It offers medicines and vaccines in various therapeutic areas, including internal medicine, vaccines, oncology, inflammation and immunology, and rare diseases. Pfizer also provides consumer healthcare products that comprise over-the-counter medicines, including dietary supplement products under the Centrum, Caltrate, and Emergen-C names; pain management products under the Advil and ThermaCare names; gastrointestinal products under the Nexium 24HR/Nexium Control and Preparation H names; and respiratory and personal care products under the Robitussin, Advil Cold & Sinus, and ChapStick names. They serve wholesalers, retailers, hospitals, clinics, government agencies, pharmacies, and individual provider offices as well as disease control and prevention centers. Over a five-year period, the company's stock price fluctuated between the low of $27.52/share and the high of $59.48/share.

Roche Holding AG (https://www.roche.com/investors/shares.htm), whose stock ticker is RHHBY, is listed on OTCQX International Premier as an American Depositary Receipt (ADR) and is headquartered in Basel, Switzerland. The company engages in the diagnostics and prescription pharmaceuticals businesses in Switzerland, Germany, and other countries. It offers pharmaceutical products for treating anemia, anticoagulation therapy, bone, cardiovascular, central nervous system, chlamydia, coagulation, dermatology, diabetes, gonorrhea, gout, hemostasis disorders, hepatitis B and C, HIV/AIDS, HPV, and inflammatory and autoimmune issues. In addition, Roche Holding AG produces intensive care medicines related to kidney and urogenital tract, leukemia, lipid and liver disorders, lymphoma, metabolic disorders, obesity, occult blood testing, ophthalmology, osteoporosis, pancreatitis, respiratory disorders, rheumatoid arthritis, sepsis, sexually transmitted infections, skin cancer, transplantation, tuberculosis, urinary tract infections, and West Nile virus and infectious diseases. The company's diagnostic solutions include blood gas analysis, blood screening, cancer screening/monitoring, cardiac markers, cardiovascular testing, cholesterol, and coagulation monitoring.

Other offerings include gene expression, gene sequencing, and real-time PCR systems for researchers. Due to their 2009 acquisition of biotech pioneer Genentech, Roche controls three of the world's top cancer drugs by sales: Avastin, for colon and lung cancers; Rituxan, for blood cancers; and Herceptin, for breast cancers. Over a five-year period, the company's stock price fluctuated between the low of $26.39/share and the high of $53.44/share.

Thermo Fisher Scientific Inc. (https://ir.thermofisher.com/investors/Investor-Overview/default.aspx), whose stock ticker is TMO, trades on NYSE and is headquartered in Waltham, Massachusetts. The company provides analytical and other instruments, laboratory equipment, software, consumables, reagents, instrument systems, chemicals, supplies, and services worldwide. Their Specialty Diagnostics segment offers liquid, ready-to-use, and lyophilized immunodiagnostic reagent kits as well as calibrators, controls, and calibration verification fluids, blood-test systems and antibody tests, products for cancer diagnosis and medical research, human leukocyte antigen typing, and testing for organ transplant market. Their Laboratory Products and Services segment offers laboratory refrigerators and freezers, ultralow-temperature freezers and cryopreservation storage tanks, temperature control, sample preparation and preservation, centrifugation, and biological safety cabinet products. The segment also offers water analysis equipment, laboratory plastics and chemicals, and pharma services. Over a five-year period, the company's stock price fluctuated between the low of $186.18/share and the high of $667.24/share.

CHAPTER FOUR

Good Price versus Good Value

The stock market is filled with individuals
who know the price of everything,
but the value of nothing.
—Phillip Fisher, world-renowned American stock investor

It is nearly impossible on face value to determine if the better investment is to buy and hold one share of a company that initially costs $400 or to buy one hundred shares of another company that costs $4 per share. It would be prudent to keep in mind the quote championed by Mr. Fisher above. The words *value* and *price* are frequently thrown around in conversations as vague connotations. We have heard the saying "Beauty lies in the eyes of the beholder." That subjectivity in identifying one's "truth" is often formulated through the narrow lenses of selective timespans, cultural preferences, and biased expectations that can cloud one's judgment. Investing can certainly be no different.

When evaluating stocks, it is critical that we apply nonsubjective metrics to evaluate whether a stock has true value, regardless of what the price currently shows. As Benjamin Graham asserted in his stellar book *The Intelligent Investor,* there is no such thing as a good stock or a bad stock. There are only cheap stocks and expensive stocks.

Even when evaluating stocks related to the highly inspirational mission of one day achieving cancer eradication, emotions (or that proverbial hunch) should never play the primary role in stock selection.

For the long-term investor (one holding a stock for at least five years) determining the value of healthcare stocks, the first metric to apply when assessing value is the price-to-earnings ("P/E") ratio. It is a basic yet fundamental yardstick that highlights the relationship between a stock's earnings (profitability) and its share price. This metric allows for apples-to-apples comparisons between companies. It measures how much an investor is willing to pay for a dollar's worth of current earnings (after-tax profits per share). Simply put, the lower the ratio, the better for the long-term investor who is buying. As my personal rule of thumb in deciding to purchase stocks, I believe that the P/E ratio should be no higher than 22 to 1 (although Benjamin Graham in his book recommended limiting oneself to stocks whose current price is no more than 15 to 1 over a three-year period).

One piece of advice to always keep in mind is this: be particularly cautious of buying any stock where the P/E ratio is significantly higher than the actual stock price, which is often the case where earnings per share is found to be less than $0.50. This provides strong warning signals of lower than desired earnings per share (as there may be other issues with a company's profitability down the road).

As much as I genuinely appreciate the P/E ratio, it can be unwise to depend solely on one metric to assess value. To complement the use of the P/E ratio, I highly recommend other metrics in assessing stock value.

> **Price/Book Value Ratio = Stock Price Divided by [Book Value - Total Liabilities]**

This metric compares the market's valuation of a company to the value that the company shows on its financial statements. The higher the ratio, the more the market is willing to pay for a company above its hard assets. As a rule of thumb, the ratio should be no higher than 1.5 when considering purchasing a stock.

> **Current Ratio = Current Assets Divided by Current Liabilities**

This "liquidity" metric tests whether a company can cover its short-term cash obligations. As a rule of thumb, the current ratio should be at least 2 to 1 when considering purchasing a stock or, at minimum, moving in that direction on a trended basis.

> **Dividend Yield = Annual Dividend/Stock Price**

This metric is particularly important when evaluating the value of a company's stock. The average dividend yield in the market is highest among real estate investment trusts (REITs), which we will discuss later in the book. Higher dividend yields are not always attractive investment opportunities as dividend yields could be artificially elevated due to declining stock prices. Such companies have an extremely high yield as their stock is falling, which usually happens before the dividend is cut. For this reason, evaluating a stock solely based on its dividend yield would be a mistake. The average dividend yield on S&P 500 index companies pays somewhere between 2 percent and 5 percent annually.

Although not a ratio, another important metric that an investor of healthcare stocks may also want to consider is beta (B), a measure of how sensitive a stock's return is relative to the return in the overall market. Beta captures that portion of an asset's risk that cannot be eliminated by diversification—also known in the academic world as systematic risk. A positive beta indicates that the return of an asset follows the general market trend. In contrast, a negative beta signifies that the return of an asset tends to move in the opposite direction of the market. A beta greater than 1.0 suggests that the stock's price is theoretically more volatile than the market; thus, on average the price of the stock moves more than the market in percentage terms. In contrast, if the price moves less than the market in percentage terms, the stock's beta is less than 1.0. For example, if the S&P 500 moved up 1 percent and your stock had a beta of 1.1, then your stock could move up 1.1 percent. If the S&P moved down 1 percent, then your stock could fall in value by 1.1 percent. In building a diversified portfolio, it would be prudent to have a mix of stocks with different betas.

The bottom line to this discussion is this: do not let the price or price trends alone be your sole guiding light in stock selections and purchases!

CHAPTER **FIVE**

Real Estate: Another Weapon Against Cancer

Don't wait to buy real estate; buy real estate and wait.
—Will Rogers, American stage and film actor, newspaper columnist, and social commentator

The best time to plant a tree was twenty years ago. The second-best time is now.
—A Chinese proverb

Although perhaps not as obvious at first when talking about fighting cancer, real estate fits like a hand in a warm glove. Real estate investment trusts, or REITs (pronounced "reets"), are companies that own or finance income-generating real estate across a wide range of property sectors. Why should you consider adding REITs to an investment portfolio related to fighting cancer? REITs are playing an ever-increasing and powerful role in the world of cancer/ oncology diagnosis, treatment, acute care, rehabilitation/trauma, and ongoing care. The growth in demand for hospital and nonhospital facilities has spurred the rocket rise in opportunities to invest in healthcare REITs that specialize in buying and leasing distinct types of healthcare facilities. These properties are, in most cases, bought by the REIT and leased back to healthcare providers who use the facilities for patient care.

REITs can be privately held or publicly traded on stock exchanges including the NYSE and Nasdaq. Because REITs do not typically operate any of their properties themselves and thus maintain exceptionally low overhead, they have the potential to generate strong returns for their shareholders over time. Investors may also purchase shares within a mutual fund or exchange-traded fund (ETF).

The history of REITs is an interesting one. They were authorized by the US Congress's Real Estate Investment Trust Act of 1960 for the deliberate purpose of providing smaller, non-institutional investors with opportunities to invest in real estate properties and, at the same time, to enjoy the same benefits provided to shareholders in investment trusts. The National Association for Real Estate Investment Trusts (NAREIT) is the premier worldwide advocate for REITs. The association provides investors with educational resources, research, data, and index information. Their website, www.reit.com, is an excellent first-stop resource for information on the diverse types of REITs in the global marketplace and how investors can participate. According to NAREIT, an estimated 87 million Americans own REITs of some type (perhaps unknowingly in their retirement accounts) across the various business sectors.

There are two basic types of REITs: equity REITs and mortgage REITs. An equity REIT is a publicly traded company that, as its principal business, buys, manages, renovates, maintains, and occasionally sells real estate properties. They also acquire and frequently develop new properties when the economic conditions are favorable. Healthcare REITs derive most of their revenue from rents by tenants according to the terms of leases that exist between the REIT (the property owner or lessor) and its tenants (the lessees). Sometimes equity REITs own properties according to a leasehold interest (also called a ground lease), in which case the REIT does not own the land on which the building sits and pays the landowner a monthly fee for an agreed-upon period (perhaps decades) in exchange for the right to use the land as needed to support the building's operations. REITs can be tax advantaged (if managed properly) in that they are not taxed at the corporate level and by law must pay out at least 95 percent of their net income as dividends to their investors. Equity REITs allow the investor to diversify not only in the type of property he or she invests in but also in the geographic location of the properties.

The second type, mortgage REIT (also called an m-REIT), is a quasi bank that lends money to real estate owners directly, by issuing mortgages, or indirectly, by acquiring existing loans, mortgage-backed securities, or other obligations that are secured by real estate collateral. They derive most of their revenues from interest received on commercial mortgage loans or from investments in residential- or commercial-based real estate instruments. The only true difference between a bank and an m-REIT and is that an m-REIT does not hold customer deposits from which to lend. Instead, they raise capital by issuing debt and equity in private or public capital markets. Their income stream in turn comprises the principal and interest payments received from these investments. We will not focus in detail on m-REITs in this book.

REITs operate under a specifically listed standard set of rules established by Congress as highlighted by NAREIT.

1. REITs must be modeled after mutual funds that give the investor the best opportunity (not guarantee) to realize the following benefits:
   - the ability to buy/sell in the open market like other stocks, mutual funds, or exchange-traded funds (ETFs)
   - the potential to obtain risk-adjusted returns given lower correlation with other stocks and bonds
   - good transparency whereby corporate governance in a REIT aligns with the shareholder's best interests

> ➤ the opportunity to receive regular dividends and generate wealth accumulation
> ➤ the potential to realize good historical returns versus S&P 500, with historically higher returns than corporate bonds

2. REITs must be treated by the IRS's Internal Revenue Code as a corporation.
3. Shareholders must widely hold REITs.
4. REITs must primarily own real estate or finance real estate as their major business.
5. At least 75 percent of the corporation's assets must be real estate.
6. At least 75 percent of the corporation's income must be earned from real estate as rent or mortgage interest income or from the sale of real estate assets.
7. At least 95 percent of REIT income must be passive income and must be passed to shareholders as taxable dividends (at ordinary tax rates to shareholders). In other words, a REIT cannot retain most of its earnings at the corporate level.
8. REITs must own real estate with a long-term investment horizon. "Flipping" (purchasing an asset with a short holding period with the intent of selling it for a quick profit rather than holding on for long-term appreciation) is not permissible.

I want to reemphasize a key characteristic of REITs. Congressional legislation exempts companies that qualify as REITs from paying corporate income tax, *provided they distribute their taxable income as dividends equal to at least 95 percent of its otherwise taxable income.* This then avoids the double-taxation issue that other corporations often face. The combination of high dividends and growth potential make healthcare REITs particularly attractive. Most specialize in several types of property subsectors, including medical office buildings, hospitals, testing facilities, life science labs, skilled nursing, and seniors housing (primarily assisted and independent living). Demand for healthcare is generally more price inelastic than other goods/services. This means that because it is often a necessity, consumers are not necessarily as sensitive to price increases. For that reason, healthcare REITs have historically been core holdings in retail and institutional investors' portfolios, especially those geared toward long-term growth. The historic stability of the healthcare sector means that healthcare REITs are viewed as more recession proof and often less risky than other types of REITs.

The most widely respected healthcare REITs have easy access to capital markets, which allows them to increase their investments by buying additional healthcare facilities or making additional mortgage loans. As lease and mortgage income received by the REIT exceeds its cost of funds (whether debt or equity), each new facility adds to free-cash flow after operations and enables the REIT to increase dividends. The highest quality healthcare REITs have well-diversified geographical locations and lessees. Another great advantage of healthcare REITs is that in a down market, they offer the protection of long-term leases with locked-in rents, while in an up market, they have lease clauses that enable them to share in the profits.

While the benefits and advantages of holding healthcare REIT assets are certainly attractive, there are risks that the investor should keep in mind. A balanced approach to investing is always a prudent exercise. With the increased demand for medical facilities, there is the possibility for oversupply arising, particularly with assisted-living and congregate-care facilities that cater to healthier (and often wealthier) senior citizens. Such facilities are not heavily regulated and do not require certificates of need before being developed. Another issue is that doctors and other healthcare providers rely on government reimbursement programs to cover their costs via reimbursement from Medicare and Medicaid. Because of this, healthcare REITs are exposed to government policy changes. If investors believe reimbursement rate cuts are possible, healthcare REIT valuations could underperform other property types. It is wise to avoid healthcare REITs that have top-heavy geographic concentration, given that nursing homes depend on state reimbursement regulations. Having too many properties in one state means exposure to the whims of that state's reimbursement policies. Therefore, bottom line, it is critical to make geographic diversification an imperative when analyzing healthcare REITs. Remember this!

Another risk to consider when reviewing healthcare REITs lies in their use of long-term, triple-net leases with the tenants who operate out of their facilities. In a rising interest rate environment, REITs that use triple-net leases tend to have returns on investment that behave and value like long-term bonds. You can recall from your old economics classes a key aspect when evaluating fixed income investments: when interest rates go up (down), the value of the asset go down (up). In a rising interest rate environment, it is possible to see your REITs underperform. Something to keep in mind.

In the following section, I have included a robust listing of publicly traded cancer-fighting REITs for you to consider in building your investment portfolio. Similar to chapter 3, I have grouped the REITs into four subsections based on the market capitalization ("cap") (stock price multiplied by the number stock shares outstanding):

Market Capitalization	
Micro Cap	Up to $300 Million (Generally Highest Stock Price Volatility)
Small Cap	Greater than $300 Million, up to $2 Billion
Mid Cap	Greater than $2 Billion, up to $10 Billion
Large Cap	Greater than $10 Billion, up to $200 Billion (Generally Lowest Stock Price Volatility)

The listing of publicly traded REITs below (provided in alphabetical order in each market cap subsection) comes primarily from general descriptions at Yahoo! Finance and/or the respective company's web sites. Please note that at the time of you reading this book, some of the companies listed below may no longer exist as distinct, stand-alone operating companies due to being acquired by another firm. We will speak briefly about M&A activities in the biotech industry in chapter 7.

Micro Cap Companies
(Up to $300 Million; Generally Highest Stock Price Volatility)

Diversified Healthcare Trust (www.dhreit.com/investors/default.aspx), whose stock ticker is DHC, trades on NasdaqGS (Global Select) and is headquartered in Newton, Massachusetts. The company owns medical office and life science properties, senior living communities, and wellness centers throughout the United States. Diversified Healthcare Trust was founded in 1998. Over a five-year period, the company's stock price fluctuated between the low of $0.92/share and the high of $19.75/share.

Regional Health Properties, Inc. (http://ir.regionalhealthproperties.com/), whose stock ticker is RHE, trades on NYSE and is headquartered in Suwanee, Georgia. The company operates through its subsidiaries as a self-managed healthcare real estate investment company that invests primarily in real estate purposed for long-term and senior living. The company's facilities offer a range of healthcare and related services to patients and residents, including skilled nursing and assisted living services, social services, various therapy services, and other rehabilitative and healthcare services for long-term and short-stay patients and residents. As of May 2019, it owned, leased, or managed twenty-eight facilities for third parties comprising approximately three thousand operational beds/units in Alabama, Georgia, North Carolina, Ohio, Oklahoma, and South Carolina. The company was founded in 1988. Over a

five-year period, the company's stock price fluctuated between the low of $0.76/share and the high of $18.60/share.

Small Cap Companies

(Greater than $300 Million, up to $2 Billion)

CareTrust REIT, Inc. (https://investor.caretrustreit.com/), whose stock ticker is CTRE, trades on NasdaqGS (Global Select) and is based in San Clemente, California. The company is a self-administered, publicly traded real estate investment trust engaged in the ownership, acquisition, development, and leasing of skilled nursing, seniors housing, and other healthcare-related properties. With a nationwide portfolio of long-term, net-leased properties and a growing portfolio of quality operators leasing them, CareTrust REIT is pursuing both external and organic growth opportunities across the United States. Over a five-year period, the company's stock price fluctuated between the low of $12.56/share and the high of $25.31/share.

Community Healthcare Trust Incorporated (https://investors.chct.reit/), whose stock ticker is CHCT, trades on NYSE and is based in Franklin, Tennessee. The company is a real estate investment trust that focuses on owning income-producing real estate properties associated primarily with the delivery of outpatient healthcare services in non-urban markets throughout the United States. Their properties include outpatient diagnostic/treatment centers, urgent care centers, acute care hospitals, ambulatory surgery centers, assisted living/long-term care facilities, medical office buildings, physicians' clinics, postacute care hospitals, and specialty hospitals and treatment centers. The company was founded in 2014. Over a five-year period, the company's stock price fluctuated between the low of $23.79/share and the high of $51.70/share.

Gladstone Commercial Corporation (https://ir.gladstone commercial.com/), whose stock ticker is GOOD, trades on

NasdaqGS (Global Select) and is based in McLean, Virginia. The real estate investment trust focuses on acquiring, owning, and operating net-leased industrial and office properties across the United States. The company invests in single tenant and multitenant net-leased assets with a diversified portfolio of over one hundred properties in more than twenty states leased to different tenants in twenty industries. Healthcare makes up approximately 20 percent of its investment portfolio. The company was founded in 2003. Over a five-year period, the company's stock price fluctuated between the low of $9.54/share and the high of $25.77/share.

Global Medical REIT Inc. (http://investors.globalmedicalreit.com), whose stock ticker is GMRE, trades on NYSE and is based in Bethesda, Maryland. The company engages primarily in the acquisition of licensed healthcare facilities and the leasing of these facilities to clinical operators with dominant market share. Their objective is to produce increasing, reliable rental revenue by leasing healthcare facilities to single-market operators (private physicians or other real estate tenants) under long-term, triple-net leases. Their view is that the net-lease operating platform tends to be more resilient during economic fluctuations. The company was founded in 2011. Over a five-year period, the company's stock price fluctuated between the low of $6.59/share and the high of $17.83/share.

LTC Properties, Inc. (http://ir.ltcreit.com/), whose stock ticker is LTC, trades on NYSE and is based in Westlake Village, California. The company is a real estate investment trust (REIT) that invests in seniors housing and healthcare properties primarily through sale-leasebacks, mortgage financing, joint ventures, and structured finance solutions, including preferred equity and mezzanine lending. The portfolio is comprised primarily of seniors housing and skilled nursing properties. LTC holds 181 investments in twenty-seven states with twenty-nine operating partners. The portfolio is comprised of approximately 50 percent seniors housing and 50 percent skilled nursing properties. The company was founded in 1992. Over a

five-year period, the company's stock price fluctuated between the low of $27.50/share and the high of $52.34/share.

Universal Health Realty Income Trust (http://www.uhrit. com/index.php/stock-quote), whose stock ticker is UHT, trades on NYSE and is based in King of Prussia, Pennsylvania. The company invests in healthcare and human service-related facilities, including acute care hospitals, rehabilitation hospitals, sub-acute care facilities, medical/office buildings, free-standing emergency departments, and childcare centers. The company was founded in 1986. Over a five-year period, the company's stock price fluctuated between the low of $41.50/share and the high of $130.30/share.

Mid Cap Companies
(Greater than $2 Billion, up to $10 Billion)

Healthcare Realty Trust Incorporated (https://www.healthcare realty.com/investor-relations/), whose stock ticker is HR, trades on NYSE and is based in Nashville, Tennessee. The real estate investment trust integrates owning, managing, financing, and developing income-producing real estate properties associated primarily with the delivery of outpatient healthcare services throughout the United States. Most of Healthcare Realty's properties are on the campuses of or next to major health systems, where they house not only essential outpatient services, such as surgery, cancer treatment, and imaging, but also key physician groups who are crucial to the hospital's long-term mission. As of July 20, 2022, Healthcare Trust of America, Inc. was acquired by Healthcare Realty Trust Incorporated in a reverse merger transaction. The company was founded in 1992. Over a five-year period, the company's stock price fluctuated between the low of $18.92/share and the high of $34.40/share.

Medical Properties Trust, Inc. (https://medicalpropertiestrust. gcs-web.com/), whose stock ticker is MPW, trades on NYSE and is based in Birmingham, Alabama. The company is a self-advised real estate investment trust formed to acquire and develop net-leased hospital facilities. The company has grown to become one of the world's largest owners of hospitals with 389 facilities and more than 41,000 licensed beds in eight countries and across three continents. The company's financing model facilitates acquisitions and recapitalizations and allows operators of hospitals to unlock the value of their real estate assets to fund facility improvements, technology upgrades, and other investments in operations. The company was founded in 2003. Over a five-year period, the company's stock price fluctuated between the low of $10.14/share and the high of $24.15/share.

National Health Investors, Inc. (NHI) (http://investors.nhireit.com/CorporateProfile/), whose stock ticker is NHI, trades on NYSE and is based in Murfreesboro, Tennessee. The real estate investment trust specializes in sale-leaseback, joint-venture, mortgage, and mezzanine financing of need-driven and discretionary seniors housing and medical investments. NHI's portfolio consists of independent, assisted and memory care communities, entrance-fee retirement communities, skilled nursing facilities, medical office buildings, and specialty hospitals. The company was incorporated in 1991. Over a five-year period, the company's stock price fluctuated between the low of $37.60/share and the high of $90.79/share.

Omega Healthcare Investors, Inc. (https://www.omegahealthcare.com/investor-relations/stock-information/stock-quote), whose stock ticker is OHI, trades on NYSE and is based in Hunt Valley, Maryland. The company is a real estate investment trust that invests in the long-term healthcare industry, primarily in skilled nursing and assisted living facilities. Its portfolio of assets is operated by a diverse group of healthcare companies, predominantly in a triple-net lease structure. The assets span all regions within the US as well as in the UK. The company was founded in 1992. Over a five-year period, the company's stock price fluctuated between the low of $22.43/share and the high of $44.96/share.

Physicians Realty Trust (https://investors.docreit.com/corporate-information/corporate-profile/default.aspx), whose stock ticker is DOC, trades on NYSE and is based in Milwaukee, Wisconsin. The self-managed healthcare real estate company was organized to acquire, selectively develop, own, and manage healthcare properties that are leased to physicians, hospitals, and healthcare delivery systems. The company conducts its business through an umbrella partnership real estate investment trust or "UPREIT," which is an alternative like-kind exchange tax benefit used to defer or completely avoid capital gains tax liability when an individual or company wants to sell appreciated real estate. In this structure, properties are owned by Physicians Realty L.P., a Delaware limited partnership (the operating partnership), directly or through limited partnerships, limited liability companies, or other subsidiaries. The company is the sole general partner of the operating partnership. Over a five-year period, the company's stock price fluctuated between the low of $12.69/share and the high of $20.74/share.

Sabra Health Care REIT, Inc. (https://www.sabrahealth.com/investors), whose stock is SBRA, trades on NasdaqGS (Global Select) and is based in Irvine, California. The company includes real estate properties (spread across the United States and Canada) that are held for investment consisting of skilled nursing/transitional care facilities, senior housing communities operated by third-party property managers pursuant to property management agreements, and specialty hospitals and other facilities. Financing programs include direct financing leasing, investments in loans receivables, and preferred equity investments. The company was founded in 2010. Over a five-year period, the company's stock price fluctuated between the low of $8.95/share and the high of $24.33/share.

Large Cap Companies

(Greater than $10 Billion, up to $200 Billion)

CBRE Group, Inc. (https://ir.cbre.com/investor-relations-home/default.aspx), whose stock ticker is CBRE, trades on NYSE and is headquartered in Dallas, Texas. The company is one of the world's largest commercial real estate services and investment firms, with a prominent global market position in leasing, property sales, outsourcing, property management, and valuation. CBRE is also the largest commercial property developer in the United States and has more than $106 billion of assets under management (AUM) within their global investors business. CBRE Healthcare is a dedicated business group within CBRE focused exclusively on supplying real estate solutions to hospitals and healthcare organizations. CBRE's healthcare valuation supplies specialized insights on healthcare and medical office and seniors housing real estate for owners, investors, and lenders. Over a five-year period, the company's stock price fluctuated between the low of $34.26/share and the high of $108.51/share.

HCA Healthcare Inc. (https://investor.hcahealthcare.com/stock_information), whose stock ticker is HCA, trades on NYSE and is based in Nashville, Tennessee. The company provides through its subsidiaries healthcare services and operates general, acute care hospitals that offer medical and surgical services, including inpatient care, intensive care, cardiac care, diagnostic, and emergency services. The company operates outpatient healthcare facilities consisting of freestanding ambulatory surgery centers, freestanding emergency care facilities, urgent care facilities, walk-in clinics, diagnostic and imaging centers, rehabilitation and physical therapy centers, radiation and oncology therapy centers, physician practices, and various other facilities. As of December 31, 2020, it operated 185 hospitals, which included 178 general, acute care hospitals as well as five psychiatric hospitals and two rehabilitation hospitals; 121 freestanding surgery centers; and twenty-one freestanding endoscopy centers in twenty states and England. Over a five-year period, the company's stock price fluctuated between the low of $76.67/share and the high of $267.00/share.

HealthPeak Properties, Inc. (https://ir.healthpeak.com/overview), whose stock ticker is PEAK, trades on NYSE and is based in Irvine, California. The company is a fully integrated REIT and S&P 500 company that owns and develops high-quality real estate in the three private-pay healthcare asset classes of life science, senior housing, and medical office, designed to provide stability through the inevitable industry cycles. The company was founded in 1985. Over a five-year period, the company's stock price fluctuated between the low of $20.29/share and the high of $37.31/share.

Ventas, Inc. (https://www.ventasreit.com/investor-relations), whose stock ticker is VTR, trades on NYSE and is based in Chicago, Illinois. The real estate investment trust holds a diverse portfolio of assets in the US, Canada, and the UK consisting of seniors housing communities, medical office buildings, university-based research and innovation centers, inpatient rehabilitation and long-term acute care facilities, and health systems. Ventas provides management, leasing, marketing, facility development, and advisory services to highly rated hospitals and health systems throughout the United States. The company was founded in 1998. Over a five-year period, the company's stock price fluctuated between the low of $21.62/share and the high of $74.56/share.

Welltower Inc. (https://welltower.com/investors/), whose stock ticker is WELL, trades on NYSE and is based in Toledo, Ohio. The company invests with seniors housing operators, postacute providers, and health systems to fund the real estate infrastructure needed to scale innovative care delivery models and improve people's wellness and overall healthcare experience. Welltower owns interests in properties concentrated in major, high-growth markets in the US, Canada, and the UK, consisting of seniors housing and postacute communities and outpatient medical properties. Many of the major global REIT exchange-traded funds (ETFs) contain holdings of the company's shares. The company was founded in 1970. Over a five-year period, the company's stock price fluctuated between the low of $37.26/share and the high of $97.82/share.

REIT Exchange-Traded Funds (ETFs)

If you have neither the time nor the patience for picking and holding individual REIT shares—or are more of a believer in diversified assets—there are a few exchange-traded funds (ETFs) that enable investors to purchase an index or bundle of REITs in a single investment that approximates the returns of the broad-based stock market index. Below are the largest REIT ETFs for you to review and consider.

First Trust S&P REIT Index Fund
Stock Ticker: FRI
Stock Market: NYSE
https://finance.yahoo.com/quote/FRI/profile?p=FRI&.tsrc=fin-srch
Contact: 1-800-621-1675

The fund seeks investment results that correspond to the price and yield (before the fund's fees and expenses) of an equity index called the S&P United States REIT Index (Ticker: STCGUSRE) that defines and measures the investible universe of publicly traded REITs domiciled in the US. The fund will normally invest at least 90 percent of its net assets (including investment borrowings) in the real estate investment trusts (REITs) that make up the index. The index seeks to measure the performance of publicly traded REITs domiciled in the United States that meet certain eligibility requirements. Major holdings include Welltower Inc. Over a five-year period, the ETF price fluctuated between the low of $16.18/share and the high of $32.60/share.

iShares Cohen & Steers REIT ETF
Stock Ticker: ICF
Stock Market: CBOE Global Markets (owner of Chicago Board Options Exchange and BATS Global Markets)
https://www.ishares.com/us/products/239482/ishares-cohen-steers-reit-etf
Contact: 1-800-474-2737

The index seeks to measure the performance of publicly traded REITs domiciled in the United States that meet certain eligibility requirements. Major holdings include HealthPeak Properties Inc., Ventas REIT Inc., and Welltower Inc. Over a five-year period, the ETF price fluctuated between the low of $39.58/share and the high of $76.08/share.

iShares Residential Real Estate Capped ETF
Stock Ticker: REZ
Stock Market: NYSE
https://www.ishares.com/us/products/239545/ishares-residential-and-multisector-real-estate-etf
Contact: 1-800-474-2737

The iShares Residential and Multisector Real Estate ETF seeks to track the investment results of an index composed of US residential, healthcare, and self-storage real estate equities. Major holdings include Healthpeak Properties, Healthcare Realty Trust Incorporated, Healthcare Trust of America Inc., Medical Properties Trust Inc., National Health Investors Inc., Omega Healthcare Investors Inc., Physicians Realty Trust, Sabra Health Care REIT, Inc. Ventas Inc., and Welltower Inc. Over a five-year period, the ETF price fluctuated between the low of $47.88/share and the high of $97.96/share.

iShares US Real Estate ETF
Stock Ticker: IYR
Stock Market: NYSE
https://finance.yahoo.com/quote/IYR?p=IYR&.tsrc=fin-srch
Contact: 1-800-474-2737

The fund seeks to track the investment results of the Dow Jones US Real Estate Capped Index that measures the performance of the real estate sector of the US equity market, as defined by the "index provider." It invests at least 80 percent of its assets in the component securities of its underlying index and in investments that have economic characteristics that are substantially identical to the component securities of its underlying index. The index seeks to measure the performance of publicly traded REITs domiciled in the United States that meet certain eligibility requirements. Major holdings include Welltower Inc. Over a five-year period, the ETF price fluctuated between the low of $60.92/share and the high of $116.14/share.

SPDR Dow Jones REIT ETF
Stock Ticker: RWR
Stock Market: NYSE
https://www.ssga.com/us/en/intermediary/etfs/funds/spdr-dow-jones-reit-etf-rwr
Contact: 1-866-787-2257

The fund seeks to provide investment results that, before fees and expenses, correspond to the total return performance of the Dow Jones US Select REIT Index. The fund invests at least 80 percent of its total assets in the securities comprising the index. The index provides a measure of real estate securities that serve as proxies for direct real estate investing, in part by excluding securities whose value is not always closely tied to the value of the underlying real estate. Major holdings include Welltower Inc. Over a five-year period, the ETF price fluctuated between the low of $62.32/share and the high of $122.16/share.

Schwab US REIT ETF
Stock Ticker: SCHH
Stock Market: NYSE
https://finance.yahoo.com/quote/SCHH/profile?p=SCHH&.tsrc=fin-srch
Contact: 1-877-824-5615

The fund seeks to track as closely as possible, before fees and expenses, the total return of the Dow Jones Equity All REIT Capped Index composed of US real estate investment trusts classified as equities. The index excludes mortgage REITs, defined as REITs that lend money directly to real estate owners and/or operators or indirectly through the purchase of mortgages or mortgage-backed securities, and hybrid REITs, defined as REITs that participate both in equity and mortgage investing. It is the fund's policy that under normal circumstances it will invest at least 90 percent of its net assets in securities included in the index. Major holdings include Welltower Inc. Over a five-year period, the ETF price fluctuated between the low of $14.01/share and the high of $26.34/share.

Vanguard Real Estate Index Fund ETF Shares
Stock Ticker: VNQ
Stock Market: NYSE
https://finance.yahoo.com/quote/VNQ?p=VNQ
Contact: 1-800-662-7447

The investment seeks to provide a high level of income and moderate long-term capital appreciation by tracking the performance of the MSCI US Investable Market Real Estate 25/50 Index that measures the performance of publicly traded equity REITs and other real estate-related investments. The advisor tries to track the index by investing all, or substantially all, of its assets directly or indirectly through a wholly owned subsidiary that is itself a registered investment company in the stocks that make up the index, holding each stock in the same proportion as its weighting in the index. The fund is nondiversified. Major holdings include Welltower Inc. Over a five-year period, the ETF price fluctuated between the low of $59.68/share and the high of $116.01/share.

CHAPTER SIX

Health Insurance Is Truly Life Insurance

There are risks and costs to a program of action. But they are far less than the long-range risks and costs of comfortable inaction.
—John Fitzgerald Kennedy, thirty-fifth president of the United States

Health insurance companies play a significant role in the fight against cancer. Given their frequently upward-sloping trajectories in corporate earnings over longer periods, these types of stocks should be included as a component of most investment strategies. Because insurance plays such an essential role as a personal financial risk management approach for most households, it also adds a nice layer of diversification within an investment portfolio. During my days of intense treatment for leukemia as a young man, I remember my father earnestly staying on top of all financial matters related to my cancer treatment. He made sure that all bills were properly processed and paid via the robust health insurance plan offered to teachers in the Indianapolis Public Schools system during that era. From that early experience onward, I came to understand and appreciate without equivocation that health insurance is truly life insurance.

Below is a listing of reputable publicly traded health insurance companies, for investing considerations, that serve the cancer-diagnosed population.

Aflac Incorporated (https://investors.aflac.com/home/default.aspx), whose stock ticker is AFL, trades on NYSE and is headquartered in Columbus, Georgia. The company provides supplemental health and life insurance products. It operates through two segments: Aflac Japan and Aflac US. The Aflac Japan segment offers cancer, medical, nursing care income support, GIFT, and whole and term life insurance products, as well as WAYS and child endowment plans under saving type insurance products in Japan. The Aflac US segment provides cancer, accident, short-term disability, critical illness, hospital indemnity, dental, vision, long-term care and disability, and term and whole life insurance products. It sells its products through sales associates, brokers, independent corporate agencies, individual agencies, and affiliated corporate agencies. Aflac offers niche products such as cancer insurance (https://www.aflac.com/prospecting/cancer-insurance.aspx) that assist with out-of-pocket medical expenses not covered by traditional health insurance. The company was founded in 1955. Over a five-year period, the company's stock price fluctuated between the low of $26.73/share and the high of $65.33/share.

Cigna Corporation (https://investors.cigna.com/home/default.aspx), whose stock ticker is CI, trades on NYSE and is headquartered in Bloomfield, Connecticut. The company's market capitalization is approximately $78 billion. Cigna provides a range of coordinated and point solution health services, including pharmacy, benefits management, care delivery and management, and intelligence solutions to health plans, employers, government organizations, and healthcare providers. The Cigna Healthcare segment offers medical, pharmacy, behavioral health, dental, vision, health advocacy programs, and other products and services for insured and self-insured customers. The company participates in Medicare Advantage, Medicare Supplement, and Medicare Part D plans for seniors as well as individual health insurance plans to on and off the public exchanges. In addition, Cigna offers healthcare coverage in its international markets as well as healthcare benefits for mobile individuals and employees of multinational organizations. The company also offers permanent insurance contracts sold to corporations to provide coverage on the lives of certain employees for financing employer-paid future benefit obligations. It distributes its products and services through insurance brokers and consultants as well as directly to employers, unions, and other groups or individuals and private and public exchanges. The company was founded in 1982. Over a five-year period, the company's stock price fluctuated between the low of $142.09/share and the high of $301.34/share.

CVS Health Corporation (https://investors.cvshealth.com/investors/default.aspx), whose stock ticker is CVS, trades on NYSE and is headquartered in Woonsocket, Rhode Island. CVS owns Aetna Inc., a premier American-managed healthcare company that sells traditional and consumer directed healthcare insurance and related services, such as medical, pharmaceutical, dental, behavioral health, long-term care, and disability plans, primarily through employer-paid (fully or partly) insurance and benefit programs and through Medicare. Since November 28, 2018, Aetna has been a subsidiary of CVS Health. Aetna's company's network includes 22.1 million medical members, 12.7 million dental members, 13.1 million pharmacy benefit management services members, 1.2 million healthcare professionals, over 690,000 primary care doctors and specialists, and over 5,700 hospitals. CVS's Health Care Benefits segment offers traditional, voluntary, and consumer-directed health insurance products and related services. As of December 31, 2021, CVS operated approximately 9,900 retail locations and 1,200 MinuteClinic locations as well as online retail pharmacy web sites, LTC pharmacies, and onsite pharmacies. Over a five-year period, the company's stock price fluctuated between the low of $52.81/share and the high of $108.49/share.

Elevance Health Inc. (formerly Anthem Inc.) (https://

ir.elevancehealth.com/stock-information/overview/default.aspx),
whose stock ticker is ELV, trades on NYSE and is headquartered
in Indianapolis, Indiana. The company's market capitalization is
approximately $112 billion. It offers a spectrum of network-based
managed care health benefit plans to large and small groups,
individuals, Medicaid, and Medicare markets. Its managed care
plans include preferred provider organizations, health maintenance
organizations, point-of-service plans, traditional indemnity plans, and
other hybrid plans. These also include consumer-driven health plans
and hospital-only and limited benefit products. The company also
provides a range of managed care services to self-funded customers,
including claims processing, underwriting, stop loss insurance,
actuarial services, provider network access, medical management,
disease management, wellness programs, and other administrative
services. In addition, it offers an array of specialty and other insurance
products and services, such as pharmacy benefits management, dental,
vision, life, and disability insurance benefits, and analytics-driven
personal healthcare. Furthermore, the company provides services to
the federal government in connection with the Federal Employee
Program and operates as a licensee of the Blue Cross and Blue Shield
Association. As of December 31, 2021, it served 45 million medical
members through its affiliated health plans. The company formerly
known as WellPoint, Inc. changed its name to Anthem, Inc. in
December 2014, followed by its most recent name change to Elevance
Health, Inc. in June 2022. The company was founded in 1944. Over
a five-year period, the company's stock price fluctuated between the
low of $191.59/share and the high of $520.67/share.

Humana Inc. (https://humana.gcs-web.com/), whose stock
ticker is HUM, trades on NYSE and is headquartered in Louisville,
Kentucky. It operates through three segments: retail, group and
specialty, and healthcare services. The company offers medical and
supplemental benefit plans to individuals. It also has a contract
with Centers for Medicare and Medicaid Services to administer the
Limited Income Newly Eligible Transition prescription drug plan

program and contracts with various states to provide Medicaid, dual-eligible, and long-term support services benefits. In addition, the company provides commercial, fully insured medical and specialty health insurance benefits comprising dental, vision, and other supplemental health benefits. It also provides administrative-services-only products to individuals and employer groups as well as military services, such as TRICARE T2017 East Region contract. Furthermore, it offers pharmacy solutions, provider services, and home solutions services, such as home health and other services, to its health plan members as well as to third parties. As of December 31, 2021, the company had approximately 17 million members in medical benefit plans as well as approximately 5 million members in specialty products. Humana Inc. was founded in 1961. Over a five-year period, the company's stock price fluctuated between the low of $230.61/share and the high of $510.54/share.

MetLife, Inc. (https://investor.metlife.com/overview/default.aspx), whose stock ticker is MET, trades on NYSE and is based in New York, New York. A financial services company, it provides insurance, annuities, employee benefits, and asset management services worldwide. It operates through five segments—US, Asia, Latin America, Europe, and the Middle East and Africa—and includes MetLife Holdings. The company offers life, dental, group short- and long-term disability, individual disability, pet insurance, accidental death and dismemberment, vision, and accident and health coverages as well as prepaid legal plans; administrative-services-only arrangements to employers; and general and separate account and synthetic guaranteed interest contracts as well as private floating rate funding agreements. In addition, it provides fixed, index-linked, and variable annuities; pension products; regular savings products; whole and term life; endowments; universal and variable life and group life products; longevity reinsurance solutions; credit insurance products; and protection against long-term healthcare services. The company also offers specific cancer insurance products (https://www.metlife.com/insurance/accident-health/cancer-insurance/). MetLife, Inc.

was founded in 1863. Over a five-year period, the company's stock price fluctuated between the low of $24.38/share and the high of $71.29/share.

UnitedHealth Group Incorporated (https://www. unitedhealthgroup.com/investors.html), whose stock ticker is UNH, trades on NYSE and is based in Minnetonka, Minnesota. The company's market capitalization is approximately $475 billion. It operates through four segments: UnitedHealthcare, Optum Health, Optum Insight, and Optum Rx. The UnitedHealthcare segment offers consumer-oriented health benefit plans and services for national employers, public sector employers, midsized employers, small businesses, and individuals. It also offers healthcare coverage and well-being services to individuals age fifty and older, addressing their needs for preventive and acute healthcare services, as well as services dealing with chronic disease and other specialized issues for older individuals. And it offers Medicaid plans, children's health insurance and healthcare programs, health and dental benefits, and hospital and clinical services.

The OptumHealth segment provides access to networks of care provider specialists, health management services, care delivery, consumer engagement, and financial services. This segment serves individuals directly through care delivery systems, employers, payers, and government entities. The OptumInsight segment offers software and information products, advisory consulting arrangements, and managed services outsourcing contracts to hospital systems, physicians, health plans, governments, life sciences companies, and other organizations. The OptumRx segment provides pharmacy care services and programs, including retail network contracting, home delivery, specialty and compounding pharmacy, and purchasing and clinical capabilities. It also develops programs in the areas of step therapy, formulary management, drug adherence, and disease/drug therapy management. The company was incorporated in 1977. Over a five-year period, the company's stock price fluctuated between the low of $206.59/share and the high of $548.32/share.

CHAPTER SEVEN

Healthcare Stocks on the Mergers and Acquisitions (M&A) Radar

Have more than you show, speak less than you know.
—William Shakespeare, iconic English poet, playwright, and actor

I love math. It's logical. It's right to the point. (Well, most of the time anyway.) The number one is always one. The number two is always two. No guesswork is needed. Despite these obvious truths, somehow in the corporate business world, basic mathematical concepts can sometimes take on an entirely different meaning where the simple equation of one plus one can equal one. Why? This occurs when one stand-alone company sends another stand-alone company's name (sometimes a well-known name), business processes, and even company culture into oblivion in the fascinating, complicated world of mergers and acquisitions (M&A).

It takes a great deal of demanding work, constant market research, and sometimes a touch of divine intuition, but if you can successfully find public firms that will soon come on the M&A radar of other companies, you could potentially reap rewards well beyond the traditional investment returns of a buy-and-hold strategy. I have benefitted quite nicely on a few occasions using this approach. Below are two examples of spectacular acquisitions in the cancer/oncology space that occurred in 2019. I will let you guess from which of these two examples I was able to take advantage of the opportunity and reap better than average returns. I'm still kicking myself for missing the other. Oh well. That's the way the game is played.

In the fourth quarter of 2019, Bristol-Myers Squibb (ticker: BMY) bought Celgene Corp for $74 billion, with a combination of cash and stock. Under the agreement, Celgene shareholders received one Bristol-Myers Squibb share and $50 cash for each share of Celgene. In addition, Celgene shareholders received one tradeable BMY contingent value right (ticker: BMY.RT) for each Celgene share. Contingent value rights entitle holders to receive additional payments for achieving future regulatory milestones. However, in the end, those contingent shares never panned out given certain milestones were not achieved, leaving the rights expiring worthless.

In 2019, the Indianapolis-headquartered pharmaceutical company Eli Lilly and Company (Ticker: LLY) completed its $8 billion buyout of Loxo Oncology, paying $235 per share in cash. The Loxo Oncology operations were attractive to Lilly because of its pipeline of targeted anticancer agents that focused on single-gene abnormalities detected by genomic testing. The tender offer represented a premium of 68 percent to Loxo Oncology's closing stock price. Loxo shares surged approximately 66.8 percent the day the news broke.

Sounds interesting?

What are some things you should keep your eye on when analyzing a company potentially on the radar of other companies? How is the company doing in terms of revenue growth? Is the P/E ratio low enough to justify another company taking a hard look? Is the company to be potentially acquired losing steam in cash flow generation? Does the company have a strong pipeline of promising new products that are protected by patents with long runways?

Ultimately could you see this company as a potential complementary strategic partner with another firm?

From time to time, it could be prudent to join in on live or recorded quarterly earnings calls of a company (you can find them on the company's investor relations pages) led by their CEO, CFO, and/or head of investor relations. Pay close attention and take notes when they speak of specific "headwinds," "new markets," or "shifts in the marketplace" related to a specific business line. These could be signals that such companies may be seeking a strategic partner who could provide them with much-needed new product pipelines to take their operations to the next profitable level.

Looking for that golden egg in the M&A space can be a hit or miss proposition, so this certainly should occupy no more than 5 to 10 percent of your investment research time. Nevertheless, this adage still exists: "You only have to be right once" to reap a lucrative payout. Seek out an investment advisory firm who could do the heavy lifting for you in terms of research. I have a particularly promising investment advisory company in mind.

Good hunting!

CHAPTER **EIGHT**

Who Can You Trust?

Good timber does not grow with ease,
The stronger wind, the stronger trees.
The further sky, the greater length,
The more the storm, the more the strength.
By sun and cold, by rain and snow,
In trees and men, good timbers grow.
**—Douglas Malloch's famous twentieth-century
metaphorical poem "Good Timber"**

People work with people they trust as they navigate the ups and downs of life. Remember the title of chapter 2: "It's Personal, and It's Business"? Investing is serious business, and it is even more serious when you are seeking to invest in profitable companies that are waging war against cancer. With that heightened sense of focus and purpose, you want to receive financial advice and put your money in the hands of those who know what they are doing and who care about you as a client. No exceptions. Placing your hard-earned funds in a company's assets under management requires trust that is backed by solid purpose and mission statements, excellent corporate governance structures, stringent financial controls, and above everything else, a track record of integrity. Tough standard? Yes. Impossible to find? Well, yes and no. Strange answer, huh?

I hope you will come to believe that there is a profoundly spiritual aspect to investing. Investing requires high confidence paired with even higher humility and integrity. The book of Proverbs from the Bible has a great deal to say about investing and trusting in others. Here are a couple of verses that set the proper context for the rest of this chapter:

> Plans fail for lack of counsel, but with many advisers they succeed. (Proverbs 15:22 NIV)

> Surely you need guidance to wage war, and victory is won through many advisers. (Proverbs 24:6 NIV)

See a common theme here? Investing is a team sport that requires trust. Thinking about investing like a lone golfer on the golf course is unwise. Thinking about investing like a soccer player or basketball player is much wiser. Players need their teammates and coaches to succeed. Yes, it is a fact that there are a few truly exceptional golfers in the world who can rise to the highest heights on their own individual abilities. However, we know that most golfers are average at best. In other words, most golfers are amateurs—paying big money to play the game—never making one red cent to play it! Ouch! Did you take personally what I just said? I hope you did. In most cases, you will not win by yourself. The stock market, like golf, often pulverizes the average, overconfident, go-it-alone type of guy or lady. You need advisors. I need advisors. Let's let that sink in.

Scholars in the academic discipline of behavioral finance have identified subconscious tendencies that often arise within investors that frequently cause them to make irrational financial decisions when such decisions are made in solitude. The most common behaviors include the following:

> ➢ **Anchoring** – The inclination to base expectations upon the first information received, which may or may not be accurate. Once a thought gets anchored in the mind, it can

be exceedingly difficult to move away from it. A first idea is not always the right idea.

> **Conservatism** – Investors often have a tough time changing their existing ingrained beliefs (often derived from childhood or early adulthood), even when new, truthful information is presented to them. An old idea is not always the right idea.

> **Herd behavior** – A market drop may be followed by panic selling. You do not want to be the last person holding the bag so you dump when everyone else dumps! A group idea is not always the right idea.

> **Overconfidence** – When investors overestimate their own ability and the accuracy of the information available to them. Hey, terrible things happen to the other guy, not to me! Right? My idea is not always the right idea.

> **Regret aversion** – The investor prepares himself or herself in such a way as to avoid distress over an adverse outcome. Think about a trip to Hawaii where you know you will in most likelihood spend more than you think but condition yourself to accept those outcomes—even when you really cannot afford to! A presumptuous idea is not always the right idea.

You are coming around, I hope (at least to a degree), to my point of view. I can almost hear the question beginning to percolate from your lips. "Eric, if I need to trust someone with my money, who should I trust?"

Here are five qualities you should strongly consider when soliciting investment advice, particularly in this specialized area of cancer/oncology investments.

1. The professional or firm is a fiduciary. That means that the company has your best interest in mind and their negotiated (preferably fee-based) pay structure reflects this.

2. The professional or firm is *not* a one-stop-shop Mr. or Ms. Know-It-All, meaning the professional or firm can connect clients with other professionals (whether lawyers, accountants, etc.) who could also provide advice, if necessary, on specific topics and could refer you without receiving any kickback commissions for doing so.

3. The investment advisory firm makes it perfectly clear to the customer whether their fees are fee based or commission based. No ambiguity is allowed!

4. The firm has a track record of presenting investment opportunities by revealing each potential company's past successes and failures. We live in an imperfect world and the stock market certainly has its moments of high volatility like any other market. Professionals or firms with integrity will share both views and would never present biased viewpoints or overpromise to impress the client. It is possible to lose money, and the client should clearly understand the risks.

5. Because we are focusing on cancer stocks, it would be wise to seek advice from a company that is closely monitoring the cancer/oncology markets for developments and changes in the biotechnology/healthcare markets.

CHAPTER NINE

Can Serve Free LLC

We can serve those investors who desire to make a profit and who have the passion to help make the world cancer free. We are Can Serve Free LLC. *Cancer free* gives life to our name and to your investment decisions.
—Eric Shea Broadus, founder and investment advisor representative, Can Serve Free LLC

Can Serve Free LLC provides fee-based investment advisory services primarily, but not exclusively, to middle income/upper income, high-net-worth individuals, small/medium size businesses, and not-for-profit organizations. The company offers these services primarily, but not exclusively, as online/automated, specialized, tailor-made investment advisory and quantitative portfolio management services related to publicly traded stocks and healthcare real estate investment trusts (H-REITs). The company operates exclusively within its business niche and expertise in helping clients find long-term, medium- to high-liquidity stock investment opportunities (via capital gains and dividends) related to cancer/oncology in the commercial areas of diagnostics, medical devices, immunotherapy, pharmaceuticals, nutrition, acute clinical care, long-term care, and real estate. The company will collaborate with clients to help them choose which types of cancer are of greatest interest to them and assist them in building specific investment portfolios of stocks and healthcare REITs related to those types of cancer. As part of the service offerings, the company will also provide educational materials and periodically host or advertise other education sessions and webinars on diverse types of cancer/oncology-related investments and healthcare real estate investment trusts.

Generally, at least forty-eight hours prior to establishing a formal business relationship requiring payment of fees, Can Serve Free LLC sends each prospective customer a client investment advisory agreement (brochure) that defines the terms, conditions, authority, and responsibilities of the company and the client. The client must return the agreement fully signed and dated prior to having further business engagements. The client investment advisory agreement with Can Serve Free LLC is nontransferable without the client's written approval. Services described in the client investment advisory agreement will entail the following:

- ➤ **Establishing an investment policy statement** – Can Serve Free LLC, in connection with the client, may develop a statement that summarizes the client's investment goals and objectives along with the broad strategies to be employed to meet the objectives. An investment policy statement includes specific information on the client's stated goals, time horizon for achieving the goals, investment strategies, client risk tolerance, and any restrictions imposed by the client.
- ➤ **Asset Allocation** – Can Serve Free LLC will develop a strategic asset allocation that is targeted to meet the investment objectives, time horizon, financial situation, and risk tolerance for each client.
- ➤ **Portfolio Construction** – Can Serve Free LLC will work, in conjunction with the input from the client, to develop a tailored portfolio that is intended to meet the stated short-term and/or long-term goals and objectives of the client.

➤ **Investment Management and Supervision** – Can Serve Free LLC will provide investment management and ongoing oversight of the client's portfolio and overall online account.

Can Serve Free LLC works with each client to identify his or her investment goals and objectives as well as risk tolerance and financial situation to create the optimal portfolio allocation. The company's business philosophy is based on modern portfolio theory ("MPT") that makes it possible for anyone who enters a Can Serve Free LLC client investment advisory agreement to access state-of-the-art investment advisory and portfolio management services. Modern portfolio theory focuses on how risk-averse investors can construct portfolios to maximize expected return based on a given level of market risk. The company's investment philosophy is grounded in the belief that markets are efficient over the long term but can become—at least temporarily—inefficient and irrational within a shorter time horizon, which requires direct investment advice to optimize finite resources.

Can Serve Free LLC tailors its investment advisory services to the individual needs of each of its clients. As a result, the company asks each prospective client a series of questions to evaluate both the individual's objective capacity and subjective willingness to take risk. The company asks subjective risk questions to determine both the level of risk an individual is willing to take and to find consistency among the answers.

Can Serve Free LLC exclusively provides investment advisory services and portfolio management services and has made the business decision—at least to this point in time—to not provide direct securities custodial services. Can Serve Free LLC will not at this time accept or maintain custody of a client's funds or securities. All client assets would be managed within brokerage account(s) of the client's choice, pursuant to the client investment advisory agreement.

At this time, Can Serve Free LLC does not participate in wrap-fee programs and does not serve as a brokerage firm and therefore will not directly manage client assets or directly trade on behalf of the client.

Can Serve Free LLC's ethical, professional, and legal duty is always to function as a fiduciary in the best interest of its clients. This means that Can Serve Free LLC puts the interests of its clients ahead of its own and carefully manages for any perceived or actual conflicts of interest that may arise in relation to its advisory services. Can Serve Free LLC will adhere to ethical standards designed to ensure that it meets its fiduciary obligations to clients, enhances its culture of compliance within the firm, and detects and prevents any violations of securities laws. Can Serve Free LLC intends to execute its business practices consistent with the code of ethics requirements of Rule 204A-1 under the Investment Advisers Act of 1940 and adhere to all applicable state and federal securities laws and specific requirements relating to, among other things, personal trading, insider trading, conflicts of interest, and confidentiality of client information.

In addition, Can Serve Free LLC provides at no charge the latest news on cancer pipeline treatments, oncology stocks, and healthcare REITs dedicated to fighting cancer from web sites such as the following (this list is not all-inclusive):

- Cure (www.curetoday.com) – articles on the latest developments in cancer care
- Dividend.com (www.dividend.com) – comprehensive dividend stock research information
- Healthcare Global (www.healthcareglobal.com)
- Hospital & Healthcare Management (www.hhmglobal.com/)
- InvestorPlace (www.investorplace.com)
- Kiplinger (www.kiplinger.com)
- Marketbeat (www.marketbeat.com)

> Morningstar (www.morningstar.com)
> REITS.org (www.reits.org)
> The Motley Fool (www.fool.com)
> TheStreet (www.thestreet.com)
> US News and World Report (www.usnews.com)

Along with providing these types of online research services, Can Serve Free LLC is structured to optimize its resources for sustainability and grow its business reputation in the years ahead in the following areas of competence and business expertise:

> **Can Serve Free Global Seed Investment Fund**
> - direct investments in global companies that manufacture and sell medical equipment related to cancer treatment
> - direct investments in heavily researched commercial real estate properties related to cancer treatment
> - direct investment in personal finance companies with expertise in providing financial planning and advisory services to cancer survivors and their families
> **Can Serve Free Giving and Corporate Partnerships**
> - charitable donations to not-for-profit organizations dedicated to cancer research, treatment, and survivorship education on a global scale
> - collaborations with certified financial planners/advisors (to provide free or heavily discounted priced financial advisory services to cancer survivors with limited incomes)
> - advise on investment bequest topics to transfer assets to others via wills
> - partner with corporations with charitable foundations
> - partner with hospitals, medical centers, and clinics

- o partner with universities and other not-for-profit organizations
- ➢ **Can Serve Free Online Store**
  - o books on cancer survivorship
  - o books on investing in the stock market
  - o books on investing in REITs
  - o Can Serve Free LLC brand merchandise for purchase and marketing purposes

Can Serve Free LLC does not and cannot guarantee any level of performance or that any client will avoid a loss of invested assets. Any investment in securities involves the possibility of monetary loss that clients should be prepared to bear. When evaluating risk, financial loss may be viewed differently by each client and may depend on different risk items, each of which may affect the probability of adverse consequences and the magnitude of any potential losses.

Please contact me at ericbroadus@canservefree.com for more information and to obtain a detailed brochure of company professional service offerings.

CONCLUSION

Nothing is more powerful than an
idea whose time has come.
—Victor Hugo, French Romantic writer and politician

The great aim of education is not knowledge—but action.
**—Herbert Spencer, English philosopher,
biologist, anthropologist, and sociologist**

A gift opens the way for the giver and ushers
him into the presence of the great.
**—Proverbs 18:16 (New International
Version of the Holy Bible)**

Now that you have finished reading every chapter in this book, I am confident that you have a much better understanding of the far-reaching impacts of cancer around the world and the plethora of investment opportunities in the cancer/oncology markets, commercial real estate markets, and health insurance markets. You understand the key criteria you should consider in selecting a competent financial advisor. At this point, I would recommend you complete two major steps before deciding to move forward with investment activities related to cancer.

Step 1: Consider your risk tolerance for investing. This should include an honest assessment of disposable cash and income available to invest, your loss tolerance (willing and able to lose X percent without selling if market turns against you), and realistic expectations for after-tax returns. Do you consider yourself a conservative investor or an aggressive investor? If you are a conservative investor, you should build a portfolio of cancer stocks with more established companies with longer histories and larger market capitalization that pay predictable periodic dividends. A more aggressive investor could forego dividends and look at younger and smaller cap companies (i.e., products still in the clinical trial stage) where the trade-offs between risk and reward are often greater.

Step 2: Make clear distinctions between objectives and constraints (limitations) to determine proper suitability for, and allocation of, your invested funds. The financial goals should clearly state what portion of your funds are reserved for income (dividends) and capital appreciation (growth) and, for the more aggressive investor, speculative investments (highly volatile stocks). Also, goals should include clear thoughts on whether to leave a portion of your investments to others as bequests (charitable gifts, inheritance, etc.). In tandem with these goals, there may be some obstacles or investment constraints that must be taken into consideration, such as time horizon (how long can your funds remain invested to ride out the ups and downs of the market), liquidity (how quickly would you need to sell stocks if cash is needed—and at what price), taxes, and preferences such as only investing in companies that are fighting particular cancers or producing a particular product.

After you have completed steps 1 and 2, I recommend you contact a financial advisory firm for assistance and discuss these two steps in greater detail. I can certainly recommend one company discussed earlier in this book without hesitation. Whether you stay with your existing financial advisor (if you have one already) or decide to choose a new firm, you should complete steps 1 and 2 above without exception.

As you recall from the introduction of this book, my story as a young man originally from Indianapolis, Indiana, highlighted how the unfair perils and consequences of leukemia powerfully, yet temporarily, derailed my early life's journey. Yet despite the earlier setbacks, the story did not end there. In a true sense, the story began there. My journey continues with a clear desire to help investors, cancer survivors, friends, family, and business professionals with their investment goals and financial aspirations. With my remaining working days on this planet, my honor and privilege would be to help you, the aspiring and successful investor, to add an exciting and potentially highly profitable new dimension to your portfolio via oncology stocks, insurance company stocks, and healthcare real estate investment trusts (REITs). We can move the time continuum toward a world that is one day cancer free while helping you generate realistic, long-term investment returns (fully cognizant and accepting of the inherent financial risks embedded in investing). Together, we can make a difference.

I really, *really* hate cancer. How about you?

I see great investment opportunities. How about you?

Let's do something about it.

Invest in cancer stocks. Make money, and make a difference.

ABOUT THE AUTHOR

Eric Shea Broadus is a leukemia survivor and the founder and investment adviser representative at Can Serve Free LLC, an investment advisory firm that specializes in helping clients find long-term, medium- to high-liquidity stock investment opportunities (via capital gains and dividends) related to cancer/oncology in the commercial areas of diagnostics, medical devices, immunotherapy, pharmaceuticals, acute clinical care, long-term care, health insurance, and real estate. Broadus holds an investment advisory license and has more than twenty years of experience in various finance roles. He earned a Bachelor of Arts degree in Economics from Indiana University-Purdue University Indianapolis (IUPUI) and a Master of Arts degree in International Relations from Johns Hopkins University School of Advanced International Studies (SAIS). He lives with his wife, Liliana, in Georgia.

Printed in the United States
by Baker & Taylor Publisher Services